$\mathcal{S}$TORYBOOK MENTORS

Grown-up Wisdom From
Children's Classics

For Her. For God. For Real.
faithfulwoman.com

Dedication

❈

With love to Scott and Brent
and to all who long to recapture the joy
of childhood as they face the realities
of a grown-up world

Bless the Lord, O my soul,
and forget not all His benefits:
Who forgives . . .
Who heals . . .
Who redeems . . .
Who crowns . . .
Who satisfies . . .
So that your youth is renewed
like the eagle's.

Psalm 103:2-5 (NKJV)

Faithful Woman is an imprint of
Cook Communications Ministries, Colorado Springs, Colorado 80918
Cook Communications, Paris, Ontario
Kingsway Communications, Eastbourne, England

STORYBOOK MENTORS
© 2001 by Brenda Waggoner

First Printing, 2001
Printed in the United States of America

1 2 3 4 5 6 7 8 9 10 Printing/Year 05 04 03 02 01

Editors: Lee Hough; L. B. Norton
Cover and Interior Design: Keith Sherrer of iDesignEtc.

Unless otherwise noted, Scripture quotations are taken from the *Holy Bible: New Internaitonal Version*®. Copyright © 1973, 1978, 1984 by International Bible Society. Used by permsision of Zondervan Publishing House. All rights reserved. Additional quotations are from *The New King James Version* (NKJV). © 1979, 1980, 1982, Thomas Nelson, Inc., Publishers; *The Message* (TM). Copyright © 1993. Used by permission of NavPress Publishing House. Verses marked TLB are taken from *The Living Bible*, © 1971, Tyndale House Publishers, Wheaton, IL 60189. Used by permission.

Some of the anecdotal illustrations in this book are true to life and are included with the permission of persons involved. All other stories are composites of real situations with names, places, and details changed to protect confidentiality.

Library of Congress Cataloging-in-Publication Data
Storybook mentors: grown-up wisdom from children's classics / [compiled by] Brenda Waggoner.
    p. cm.
  ISBN 0-7814-3502-1
    1. Children's literature--History and criticism. 2. Children's literature--Moral and ethical aspects. I. Waggoner, Brenda.

PN1009.A1 S845 2001
809'.89282--dc21

                                               00-051396

Contents

Foreword

If, as a young girl, you loved going to the library almost as much as going on a date, if the friends in your favorite book were almost as real as the friends in your neighborhood, if you loved the smell of leather and bookbinding, then you now hold in your hands a treasure that will bring back the happiest moments of childhood. And if you missed the childlike joy of reading *Black Beauty* or *Make Way for Ducklings* or *Anne of Green Gables*—well, have I got good news for you: it's never too late to have a happy childhood. And we never outgrow the timeless wisdom in classic children's stories.

As I read through the manuscript of *Storybook Mentors,* I realized that even as a grown-up I have much to learn and relearn from the creative mystique of Mary Poppins, the vivid imagination of Anne Shirley, and the self-sacrifice of one beloved spider named Charlotte. Jesus, the Gospel of Mark declares, was "never without a story when he spoke." Perhaps Christ knew that the best way to sneak into hardened hearts was through the back door of a good story. For who can resist a bit of adventure or eavesdropping on some sparkling conversation? So stories become our teachers. And if the story is rich and deep, if it teaches us—scene by unfolding scene—to be kinder and gentler and braver people, then we have been mentored well.

So head to a window seat or rocker or porch swing with a copy of *Storybook Mentors* and discover again—or for the very first time—some of the most well-loved books and characters of our time.

Thank you, dear Brenda, for opening your tender heart to us once again in this book, which is destined to be a classic in its own right.

Becky Freeman
Author and speaker
(www.beckyfreeman.com)

Acknowledgments

In appreciation of authors of the best-loved children's classics, who have enriched so many lives over the years.

Heartfelt thanks to Lee Hough, product manager at Cook Communications, for his sensitivity to the difficult realities of life, for his commitment to producing quality literary works, and for his help in conceptualizing, structuring, and guiding this project from beginning to end. Thanks also to L.B. Norton, editor, and others at Cook Communications who worked on editing, layout, and design, to help make this book what it is.

Sincere thanks and appreciation to Becky Freeman and Gracie Malone, mentors, fellow authors, friends. Especially for our "writers trio" lunches, when we mix small bits of business with generous helpings of interesting conversation and fun. Thanks also to Ruthie Arnold for last-minute editing help.

Thanks to the many people who have influenced my life—family, friends, children, authors I have loved. This book really belongs to them, because many of their thoughts are shared here. Thanks also to my clients, who never cease to inspire me with their courage. Their stories enrich my own life and increase my faith in Christ more than I can say.

I offer my love and gratitude to my sons, Scott and Brent Whitson, who shared with me the joy of their childhood. I also appreciate their allowing me to tell some of their personal stories.

Thanks to my husband, Frank, for love, encouragement, and for sharing childlike joy with me in our grown-up life. He has helped me learn to slow down and notice the little things in life—flowers, birds, and other expressions of God's creativity. Frank embodies, more than any adult I know, the spontaneity and winsome nature of a child.

In special recognition of Dr. Coyle Stephenson, whose biblical insights and observations of human nature have added depth and purpose to my life, my counseling practice, and my writing.

Introduction

All the great stories get their start as children's stories. That's because when we're children we're discovering the world from the ground up. We're working with the basics. And no matter how long we live, no matter how mature we become, we're never removed from the basics.[1]

Eugene Peterson, *Leap Over a Wall*

What were your favorite classic stories during your growing-up years? As a little girl, did you often "escape" for an entire weekend, burying your nose in a book? Which stories did you savor over and over, tucked into a cozy bed, or curled up in a stack of pillows on a lazy afternoon? Who were the main characters—the mentors—who embodied traits you wanted to emulate? The wonderful childhood world of imagination, pretend, and creativity held its own kind of magic. Animals talked. People could fly. We counted on happy endings.

By the time we cross the threshold of adulthood, we've all collected our share of life's scars and bruises. As grown-ups we find the magic formulas we once believed in don't always add up to an ideal life. So we begin sorting through the skills we've collected along the way, keeping those that still benefit us and discarding the ones that are no longer useful. We learn that some stories don't have happy endings. Pretending doesn't work in the adult world. Yet creativity and imagination add depth and adventure to our lives at any age. Knowledge enriches life, but if we become too sophisticated on our way to this thing we call "maturity," we lose the spontaneous joy and sense of wonder that came so naturally to us as children.

When we were small, we had no problem embracing the heroism of a horse called *Black Beauty* or the generosity of *The Giving Tree*. Even for adults, I believe there are valuable lessons to be learned from these beloved characters, deeper truths to be discovered by revisiting these classic tales. As women, we try so hard to live well. Yet, even with our sizeable knapsacks of life experience and analytical knowledge slung over our shoulders, we often find that becoming wiser, more joyful, more like Christ, eventually takes us back to becoming more like children.

When we boil all our knowledge down and distill it into simple truths, the lessons we learned as little girls have not been improved upon. I would even say that themes taught by our childhood heroes and heroines have great biblical significance, since all virtue originates in the character of God. Jesus tells us, "Become like children." Perhaps it is only through the perception of a child that we understand with the heart, know without question we are precious to our Father, and accept God's love with open arms. If we're on our way to becoming more childlike in our quest for "maturity," it seems a worthwhile pastime to look again at classic literature written especially for children.

Are you ready for a heartwarming adventure? Let's revisit some classic *Storybook Mentors* together. In the first section of the book, we'll greet some mentoring children, since it seems appropriate to begin there. Then we'll move on to stories about wise friends, and conclude with lessons from elders. Just in case you haven't read the classic in a while, or perhaps missed it altogether, I've included a summary (*Crux of the Classic*) at the beginning of each chapter.

Perhaps a mentor's wisdom grows up along with us, over the years. Then again, maybe we just see more clearly as adults when we look at the world through a child's eyes. The only thing I'm sure of is that the valiant heroism of classic mentors hasn't changed a bit, and their simple truths still apply as much as ever to our lives.

Brenda Waggoner

We turn, not older with years, but newer every day.[2]
Emily Dickinson

timeless stories

of

CHILDREN asMENTORS

Anne of Green Gables

A Little Princess

Heidi

Pippi Longstocking

Pollyanna

chapter one

*I*MAGINATION

"I'm going to imagine that I am the wind that

is blowing up there in those treetops.

When I get tired of the trees I'll imagine

I'm gently waving down here in the ferns . . .

and then I'll go with one great swoop over

the clover field—and then I'll blow over the

Lake of Shining Waters and ripple it all

up into little sparkling waves."

Anne Shirley

Anne of Green Gables

by L.M. Montgomery

When Matthew Cuthbert arrived at the train station in Bright River to pick up an orphan boy (hoping to get some help with the heavy farm chores), he found a girl awaiting him instead. Her name was Anne Shirley, and she'd been dropped off at the station by an orphanage attendant. Anne dearly hoped to be adopted by Matthew and his spinster sister, Marilla. She'd spent a great deal of time imagining her new home with the Cuthberts at Green Gables, and hoped with all her heart she'd never have to return to the orphanage.

"I'm not expecting a girl," said Matthew to the stationmaster. "It's a boy I've come for."

"Guess there's some mistake," the attendant replied. "That girl . . . said you and your sister were adopting her."

Matthew was a shy man with a kind heart, and he didn't know what to do. He knew Marilla (who was definitely the boss around the house) wouldn't take kindly to his bringing home a girl. But Anne looked so sad and homely, Matthew decided she could at least spend the night at Green Gables while he and his sister thought things over.

On Anne's first night there, Marilla tucked her into bed, instructing her to say her prayers. "What am I to say?" asked Anne, who had never said a prayer before. Marilla soon saw Anne's dire need of mothering and instruction. So the Cuthberts decided to keep Anne Shirley, even though she wasn't a boy.

Right from the start, Anne's perky personality added strokes of color to life at Green Gables, keeping Matthew and Marilla guessing what she'd say, do, or imagine next. At eleven years of age, Anne was a skinny, freckle-faced girl with bright red hair and big gray eyes that were alive with mischief. But the liveliest thing of all about Anne was her vivid imagination. Sometimes she even imagined that her carrot-colored hair (which she hated) was raven black.

One of the first neighbors Anne met at Green Gables was Mrs. Rachel Lynde, who came to inspect the Cuthberts' new boarder. The instant Mrs. Rachel laid eyes on Anne, she blurted out, "Lawful heart, did anyone ever see such freckles? And hair as red as carrots!"

"I hate you!" shouted Anne, with no consideration of the consequences her impulsive words might evoke. "How dare you say I'm freckled and red-headed! How would you like to . . . be told that you are fat and clumsy and probably hadn't a spark of imagination in you?" To Anne, having no imagination was a very serious character flaw.

Of course Anne was scolded by Marilla, sent to her room, and told she'd have to stay there until she apologized to Mrs. Rachel. When Marilla wasn't around, Matthew sneaked by Anne's little bedroom to check on her. "How are you making it?"

"Pretty well," said Anne. "I imagine a good deal, and that helps to pass the time."

Matthew, knowing his determined sister wasn't about to relent, persuaded Anne to go ahead and get the apology over with. The next day Marilla took Anne to Mrs. Rachel's house, where Anne delivered a dramatic declaration of repentance.

"Do you never imagine things different from what they really are?" Anne asked Marilla, once the incident with Mrs. Rachel was settled.

"No," came the no-nonsense reply. "If you'll be a good girl you'll always be happy."

But Anne responded in a meditative discourse, as she so often did: "I'm going to imagine that I'm the wind that is blowing up there in those treetops. When I get tired of the trees I'll imagine I'm gently waving down here in the ferns—and then I'll fly over to Mrs. Lynde's garden and set the flowers dancing—and then I'll go with one great swoop over the clover field—and then I'll blow over the Lake of Shining Waters and ripple it all up into little sparkling waves. Oh, there's so much scope for the imagination in the wind!" Then Anne promised to stop talking so much, and Marilla breathed a sigh of relief.

As Anne grew older, she became the light of Matthew and Marilla's lives, and she also won great affection in the community. At fifteen, she qualified to study at Queen's Academy. As Matthew reflected on the circumstances that had brought Anne to them, he said, "She's been a blessing to us, and there never was a luckier mistake. . . ."

When Matthew died suddenly, Anne made the sacrificial decision to give up her academic career to stay at Green Gables, teach at the local school, and help Marilla keep the farm. But things worked out fine, as they always seemed to for Anne. The joys of having people to love, a home, genuine friendships, and an imaginative mind were hers. To Anne, it seemed that was about all any girl had a right to ask for. [1]

There were seemingly no bounds to the imagination of Anne Shirley. She could picture almost anything in her head, and she often used this ability to get her through the hardest of times, envisioning a better life for herself, imagining a home and family, seeing herself as a winner. In this chapter we'll consider the value of picturing things in our minds, even as adults, and Anne will be our guide.

The world of imagination—a close cousin of faith and hope—can go a long way toward enhancing life at any age. Imagination adds depth to the spiritual life of adults, enabling them to picture biblical truths in their minds, enlivening their walk with God.

It was imagination that C.S. Lewis employed to draw teachings about real life from fantasy, helping readers picture and understand biblical truths played out in story form. Personifying good and evil through imaginative characters, Lewis has taken children and grown-ups alike on fantastic adventures of scriptural significance in his highly acclaimed Chronicles of Narnia. My husband reads them at least once every two years, and I can always tell when he's deeply engrossed in one of the tales. He's more lively. More adventuresome. More descriptive in his language—as if the words on the pages have actually drawn Narnian pictures in his head!

In *The Sacred Romance*, authors Brent Curtis and John Eldredge say that in the church today we need to rediscover a "way of seeing" God.[2] Although we may have thoroughly mastered biblical study skills, and we know how to analyze text and process information, we've lost the ability to see God in everyday life. Do you ever bring your imagination into your spiritual life, offering your mind to God in such a way, picturing scriptural truths in your head?

A woman named Sally learned to envision something that would enrich her life, a truth she was praying for, by using the same picturing power of her mind that Anne Shirley used.

PICTURING TRUTH IN YOUR MIND

Sally was in her mid-thirties, and she wanted to rely on God as she dealt with her infant son's recent death. At two weeks of age, the premature baby boy had caught a rare virus and stopped breathing. His minimal birth weight of just a tad over five pounds hadn't helped. Try as they did, the doctors could not revive Sally's son. Some weeks passed, and Sally was still in the process of grieving her catastrophic loss, searching for some way to see God's involvement in this emotional struggle.

"I know the Bible says my little Stevie is in heaven now," said Sally, perhaps trying to convince herself as well as me. "To be absent from one's body here is to be present with the Lord in Spirit." Sally had been a Christian since her teenage years, and she knew a lot of scriptural truths. But now her beloved child had gone on to that mysterious place in the sky. There were no concrete eyewitness accounts describing exactly what heaven was like, but with her son there, Sally felt a more intense need to understand what her son's new dwelling place might look like, feel like, sound like.

"What is heaven like?" she asked desperately one day in my counseling office, wringing a Kleenex with her hands. Though I could have ventured a guess, I knew my interpretations of eternity were not what she needed. And I doubted Sally would find much solace from facts, true though they were. Oftentimes, especially in matters of the spiritual realm, more direction is given my clients as a result of our mutual prayer than from any advice I might offer.

During the next few weeks Sally read passages from the Bible describing heaven, and she checked out a couple of books from her church library on the subject. Time passed. Then one day as Sally entered my office, I noted a visible change in her countenance. "Wait until I tell you what has helped me!" she exclaimed.

"I read everything I could find in the Bible about heaven," she went on to explain, "but I needed a way of picturing where my Stevie is now. One day when I was missing him so badly, I just closed my eyes and tried to see him in the arms of Jesus. And all of a sudden, it didn't matter what heaven looked like. It didn't matter at all. I just pictured my Stevie being lovingly cared for by Jesus, safe in His arms, and that's all I needed."

Sally hadn't found much encouragement in just trying to absorb information about heaven. But by using her imagination, God's Spirit revealed to her a deeper kind of knowing the whereabouts of her little son, forever absent from her in this life, but present with the Lord in eternity. As she sat alone with God, using her mind to picture a spiritual truth, she felt comforted and peaceful.

> *Instead of taking the words apart, we should bring them together in our innermost being; instead of wondering if we agree or disagree, we should wonder which words are directly spoken to us and connect directly with our most personal story.*[3]
>
> *Henri Nouwen*

WORD PICTURES IN THE SCRIPTURES

I spent the first twenty years of my Christian life concentrating on acquiring Bible knowledge and praying the same verbal prayers over and over in list form, with slight variations. Reading the Scriptures and praying are indeed important elements of the Christian life. But at some point it seemed God was calling me into a different way of encountering His Word as I read, bringing Spirit-led imagination into my devotional life.

It was quite unlike the way I'd read or studied in the past. It wasn't something I practiced *instead of* studying the Bible; rather, I began to conclude my morning devotional readings by slowing down a bit, mixing words from the Bible with prayer. I'd take a verse, or even just one phrase, and hold it in my mind, with my eyes closed, letting the words freely take their own direction, sinking into my heart or drawing pictures in my head as I sat still and quiet. It was more like the words were reading me than I was reading the words.

In his book *Living Prayer*, author Robert Benson talks about the traditions of prayer, including "mental prayer," which the contemplatives teach. I'd read a few books about contemplative prayer, but most of them were so far over my head, I got dizzy just trying to understand the concepts. But Benson described deep concepts in simple terms, and they made sense to me. Without knowing it, I'd stumbled over *lectio divina*, a term that has to do with reading and prayer. Benson explains,

> *You begin by reading a scripture passage slowly, aloud perhaps, once or twice or three times. Then you imagine yourself in the setting of the scripture itself. You see yourself as the different characters in the story or the setting, you listen to the sounds that emanate from it, touch its textures, smell its smells, feel its tensions. Then you begin to listen for what it is saying to you, making notes if you think to . . . or simply sit and say a phrase over to yourself.*[4]

Reading and praying the Scriptures pictorially, imaginatively, requires more trust, because I must abandon myself to the process without regard for results. I was taught to come at the Bible only with my intellect, and I feel much safer when I am in control of the process. This way of reading invites the imagination to take an active part in the encounter. For me, it makes the verses more lifelike, as if I am actually interacting with the characters in that moment, taking part in the scene. I am not merely absorbing information, making notes, or charting a section of text.

The mysteries of the spiritual life are beyond what we can diagram. They're more about releasing control than hanging onto it. Inviting God's presence to direct both our intellect and our imagination can take us beyond ourselves.

In the Scriptures, we see many examples of Jesus inviting us from the place where we find ourselves, to discover eternal truth through use of imagination. He often did this by telling parables. "The kingdom of heaven will be like ten virgins who took their lamps and went out to meet the bridegroom," Jesus said (Matthew 25), instructing people to be ready for His coming. Using familiar terms and expressions of the day, Jesus encouraged people to picture in their minds the kingdom of heaven, and what it might look like to make their preparations.

The psalmist often painted word pictures with strokes of colorful metaphor and imagery. In Psalm 1, a righteous man is sketched as a tree planted by streams of water, yielding fruit in season; a wicked man as chaff, blown away by the wind. The psalmist also spoke repeatedly of meditating—seeing (mentally picturing) scriptural truths in the midst of life.

When we refer to meditation, what we sometimes mean (at least this was once true for me), is thinking about a passage for five minutes or so, scanning for some surface meaning. Then we'll have something to say at our next Bible study meeting, some important insight to share that will make us look good. But the whole point of meditating, as the psalmist meant it, is to receive *for ourselves* a soul-nourishing truth from God. It's not something we're planning to tell about, write about, or use in any way. Rather, meditation is God's creative gift, a way of strengthening us by enabling us to picture Him in the midst of life, within the safe limits of scriptural truth.

———— ∞ ————

"I'm going to imagine that I am in the wind that is blowing up there in those tree-tops," said Anne of Green Gables, picturing in her mind what it might be like to be the wind blowing in the ferns or dancing with the flowers in Mrs. Lynde's garden or blowing rippling waves over the surface of a lake. *"Oh, there's so much scope for the imagination in the wind!"*

If we can catch the wisdom of our storybook mentor, it may serve us well as we strive to follow Christ. *"I'm going to picture myself entering into Heaven's gates as the bride of Christ on my wedding day,"* I might say. *"Oh, there's so much scope for the imagination within the truths of God's Word!"*

In your life today, what scriptural truth do you need to see? Does it have to do with envisioning yourself completely forgiven by God? Find a biblical passage and try picturing it in your mind. Like Sally, you may need to find a "way of seeing" Christ's presence with a loved one in heaven. Or you may find yourself in the midst of a trial, as my friend Gracie did shortly after a back surgery, searching for a "way of seeing" God.

Six weeks after Gracie's operation, she had to admit that her six-inch surgical scar was still fiery red with inflammation. She'd been told that a serious infection was threatening to invade bone mass in her back, making further surgery inevitable.

The night before her surgery, Gracie lay in her hospital bed trying not to panic. After an hour or so of fitful tossing, she called John, a friend and counselor. At the time of her phone call, John happened to be reading Psalm 23. John suggested she listen to the pastoral words, thinking they might calm her frazzled nerves.

"The Lord is my shepherd," John read as Gracie closed her eyes and listened at the other end of the phone line. "I shall not want. He leads me beside still waters. He restores my soul. His rod and staff comfort me."

Then John stopped reading and said, "Now I want you to go to sleep, Gracie. And as you drift off, I want you to visualize the Good Shepherd standing right beside you. Beside Him are two sheepdogs. Their names are Goodness and Mercy. As you sleep tonight and as you go into surgery tomorrow, Goodness and Mercy will be following you."

As Gracie drifted off to sleep, the mental picture of those two sheepdogs gently covered her with a fleecy-soft blanket of peace.

"When I awoke after the surgery," Gracie concluded, "I still remembered that Goodness and Mercy had never left my side."

wisdom of old

The crisis . . . that afflicts the church today is a crisis of imagination.[5]

Brent Curtis & John Eldredge

Jesus knew that the adults He taught would have a lot more trouble picturing the realities of His kingdom than would the children who clambered into His lap. As we mature, we learn to think abstractly, developing analytical skills. But nothing will ever erase the need we have to soak in the foundational, peace-bringing truths of Christ's love for us, His sons and daughters, to let them seep down into our hearts as we picture ourselves embraced in His arms. Yet how often we collect spiritual truths and line them up like rows of soldiers in our heads, only bringing them out to defend a theological point!

As we have already noted, our Lord often used parables to teach His disciples and others, likening spiritual fruitfulness to the planting of seeds, or the kingdom of heaven to a treasure hidden in a field. I'm sure His reasons for teaching in word pictures and analogies are far beyond my ability to comprehend or explain, but I can't help but note His use of everyday, familiar concepts. Jesus spoke to people in terms they could relate to.

Still, even when Jesus used simple analogies, grasping the meaning of a parable wasn't easy for those without tender hearts. It was the scholars of the day, the Pharisees, who had the most trouble understanding His simple stories. They were only concerned with knowing black-and-white facts and keeping every jot and tittle of the law. Anne Shirley would have been appalled by their absolute lack of capacity for imagination!

In Matthew 13, the disciples came and asked Jesus, "Why do you tell stories?" He replied, "You've been given insight into God's kingdom. You know how it works. Not everybody has this gift. . . . That's why I tell stories: to create readiness, to nudge the people toward receptiveness"

(Matthew 13:11, TM).

God, through the Holy Spirit, uses a variety of ways to reveal previously hidden truths to His children, including running a parade of pictures through our minds, if He so chooses. As the author of creativity, He has unlimited resources at hand to unveil truth to us, even as grown-ups, giving us eyes to see. Sometimes He takes us back to a state of childlikeness, waking up our imagination. He may draw us to Himself through the use of word pictures, poetry, nature, or an unlimited array of other ways, to help us picture His truths in our minds.

The Bible is always our plumb line of truth, and by it we can test our imaginations. Beyond that, it's really not for us to say how God will reveal spiritual truths. All we can do is keep offering ourselves to Him, seeking Him, asking for eyes to see things as He says they are.

"Do you never imagine things different from what they really are?" Anne asked Marilla, soon after her arrival at Green Gables.

"No," came the flat reply.

"Oh!" cried Anne. "Oh, Marilla, how much you miss!"

But these lines are spoken early in the story. Anne's penchant for picturing life at its best has even rubbed off on Marilla by the time we reach the end of the book. And my sincere hope is that you, too, have been "nudged toward receptiveness," as Jesus said, seeking eyes that see—really see.

c h a p t e r   t w o

*H*OPE

"*It would be easy to be a princess*

if I were dressed in cloth of gold,

but it is a great deal more of a

triumph to be one all the time."

Sarah Crewe

A Little Princess

by Frances Hodgson Burnett

This tale of riches to rags to riches is about Sara Crewe, a winsome child who once lived in a mansion in India. Sara never knew her mother, who had died when she was born, though she did have a locket with her picture inside. Sara's only relation in the world was her young, handsome, rich father (whose picture was also kept in the locket). Sara and her father always played together and loved each other dearly. But the climate of India was thought to be bad for children, so when she was seven years old, Sara was sent away to an English boarding school.

When Sara's father suddenly died, she was left penniless and at the mercy of Miss Minchin, the vindictive headmistress. Miss Minchin quickly and coldly turned Sara into a servant and forced her to live in the attic and dress in rags. She was no longer allowed to play and talk freely with the other girls at the school. But it was here in the attic that Sara met Becky, a scullery maid who became her dear companion.

Sara missed her father terribly. On the bleakest of days, she kept her spirits up by remembering him and clinging to the knowledge that he loved her very much. She often spoke of her father, though not around Miss Minchin.

Sara also had other ways of trying to make her fatherless life bearable. She began to hold secret meetings in her attic bedroom, telling the girls at the school beautiful stories of magical faraway places. This kept her mind off her miserable circumstances, at least for a while. Sometimes she talked to her favorite doll as if it were real, and made friends with birds and rats. Sara did all she could to lift her own spirits, as well as those of others, by pretending she lived in a better world. To Sara, all of life was a story.

But at times her sadness nearly overcame her. During the happy days with her father, when she'd been dressed in clean clothes every day and spent time playing with her friends, it was easy to remember she was a little princess, as her father called her. But now that she dressed in rags, slept in a cold attic, and often went hungry, things were different. Miss Minchin declared Sara a destitute beggar, and sometimes it was all the little girl could do to keep from believing it.

"It has been hard to be a princess today," said Sara, on one of her gloomier days. "It would be easy to be a princess if I were dressed in cloth of gold, but it is a great deal more of a triumph to be one all the time." More than anything, Sara wanted to keep believing that no matter what happened, she was still a little princess.

Eventually a mysterious benefactor, Mr. Carrisford, who lived next door to the boarding school, noticed Sara's hopeful attitude and good behavior in the midst of grave living conditions. He began to watch her, and observed that "she had the bearing of a child who were one of the blood of kings." After questioning her, Mr. Carrisford realized Sara was in fact the daughter of his beloved friend and former business partner, the late Captain Ralph Crewe. For two years, Mr. Carrisford had been searching for the child, inquiring at all the schools in Paris and London. All the while, Sara had been right next door.

Sara's former life of wealth and riches was then restored as she went to live with Mr. Carrisford, and Becky became her happy and gracious attendant. Whether Sara was dressed in rages or riches, she learned that she could always be a princess on the inside.[1]

mentor's wisdom

Which one of us can't find a few things in common with Sara Crewe? Did you ever make believe you lived in a better world when you were a little girl? Did you talk to your dolls, pretending they were real live friends? I had a special doll named Sweet Sue during my growing up years. I carried her around, talked to her, and set a place for her at the kitchen table. She even had her very own cup and saucer. In many ways, Sweet Sue was a lifelike friend during those childhood days.

What kind of pretend games did you play when you were a little girl? The world of make-believe is a healthy, normal part of our play, as well as a natural way of coping with difficulties. But by the time we've reached adulthood, we find that pretending, once such a powerful and effective tool, no longer works. What a disappointment this can be.

Sometimes we may stubbornly cling to pretending, trying to make it work as it did during childhood. (Adults call this denial.) In *A Little Princess*, Sara Crewe wasn't old enough to get involved in the games adults sometimes play. But as we grow into adulthood and life brings its share of disappointments, we women sometimes opt for denial instead of squarely facing our grown-up realities. Perhaps we imagine that problems

27

in our marriage will magically disappear without any effort or growth on our part. Or maybe we pretend we're happy to add just one more responsibility to our job description, when we know we're already overworked and battling resentment. More often, it happens subtly, and we're not really aware we're still pretending.

Then what are we to do? you may be wondering. *If we have to stare the cold, hard realities of the adult world in the face, how can we remain hopeful?* Excellent question. I hear it often in my counseling office.

In this chapter, we'll try to learn a few things from Sara Crewe. Sara was separated from her beloved father at the time of his death, and from that point on, she was treated as an unwanted beggar child. But Sara knew that her life was a story, and through all her difficult experiences, she tried hard not to let circumstances define who she was. Even when she was treated as an outcast, she remained hopeful by remembering that she was still her father's little princess.

A STORY LARGER THAN MAKE-BELIEVE

It is only when we see God as the Hero of the larger story that we come to know his heart is good.[2]

Brent Curtis & John Eldredge

In our lives as women, just as in Sara Crewe's life, there's a larger story going on than the one defined by our immediate circumstances. The larger story is a true rags to riches story about your Heavenly Father, who calls you His beloved daughter. As the man Christ Jesus, He died for you, so that you could spend eternity with Him in heaven. He loves you. He invites you to be His daughter in the larger story—the one with meaning far beyond today's circumstances, whatever they may be. Perhaps you're in the midst of a divorce, you feel like a reject, and you now define yourself as a divorcée. Or you're recovering from bankruptcy and you think of yourself as a financial loser. Maybe both of your parents have died, and you see yourself as an orphan.

Though we may get caught up in the plots of our own lives, letting what's happening to us define who we are, our Heavenly Father never forgets the larger story—His story. He offers us hope through our inheritance as His beloved princesses—we are members of the royal lineage, precious, and bought at great price. In exchange for the dirty rags of abuse, shame, divorce, slander, the results of our poor choices, He offers the riches of heaven itself. This is the never-changing theme of the larger story, the true story of your life.

Just as Sara Crewe tried hard to remember she was a little princess whether dressed in rags or riches, we must cling to the truth of our inheritance even in the midst of life's cruelest realities. To remember that we are little princesses is not the same as pretending. Quite the contrary. It's simply maintaining hope because we belong to God.

Sometimes the lines between reality and pretending are not so clear. Even as adults, we can be subtly drawn back into a game of pretend unaware. *What would that look like in a woman's life?* you may wonder. *Why would we go on pretending, even when we're grown women?* Let's take a closer look at pretending, that wonderful game that worked so well for us as little girls, and see if we can discover why we sometimes cling to it as adults.

At thirty-nine, Maggie was finally expecting the baby she and her husband, Jeff, had hoped for since they'd married in their mid-twenties. Because of Maggie's age and the fact that she was Rh negative, the doctor had advised the couple not to have any more children after this. Although both Maggie and Jeff wanted a larger family, they accepted as God's providence the fact that this would be their only child.

Three weeks before Maggie's delivery date, she was doing some chores around the house when intense pains struck her lower abdomen, sending her staggering to the floor. Maggie managed to crawl to the phone and call Jeff at work. Thirty minutes later, the couple arrived at the hospital emergency room.

The next week I heard the sad news that Maggie and Jeff's baby had suffocated before passing all the way through the birth canal, arriving stillborn. "Oh, no, I'm so sorry," I whispered into the telephone receiver when Janet, a neighbor of Maggie's, called asking friends to pray.

"Me too," Janet replied. "This baby is all Maggie and Jeff have talked about for months, all they've planned for, prayed for, hoped for."

The very next Sunday, I was surprised to see Maggie at church. Jeff wasn't there, but Maggie appeared to be taking things in stride, even volunteering to teach a third-grade Sunday School class the next quarter.

"Maggie, how are you?" I asked, stopping her in the hallway just before the service began.

"Oh, I'm fine, Brenda, really just fine," she said, forcing a tense smile. "How's your life going these days?"

"Maggie, I'm so sorry about your baby," I said, trying to make eye contact as she looked over my shoulder at a group of women friends.

"Oh, I'm doing great! There's Sally!" said Maggie, ignoring my attempt to console. "I've got to go ask her something. See you later!" As Maggie scurried down the hall, I noticed she did not approach Sally, who was talking with two other friends, but instead headed toward the ladies room.

Would any of us really blame Maggie for pretending she was just fine? How devastating it must have been to have prayed for a baby more than a decade, to finally get pregnant near the end of her childbearing years, and then to lose the child during the birthing process. How empty her heart must have felt. How unspeakably sad the moment of her only child's death must have been for her.

When the wounds of life cut deepest, facing reality may hurt so much that we embrace an escape just to find shelter from some of the pain. It's understandable, and we all do a little pretending now and then. But over the long haul, once we've grown into women, something within us will no longer accept make-believe as a way of life. If we try to keep it up, we feel unsettled inside, we find no peace.

As women, we all long to know we are somebody's princess. Like Sara Crewe, we want to be the apple of our Father's eye. For a few, that dream will reach some level of fulfillment through a couple relationship that just seems to flow easily, naturally, almost effortlessly. But even the best of marriages in this life are but a fleeting glimpse of the perfect love our Heavenly Father has for us. Sooner or later, all human relationships will let us down. If we focus merely on immediate circumstances, our lives will follow a roller coaster path, alternating between the highs of joyful events and the lows of problems and tragedies.

We must learn to look beyond today's chapter of party dresses or dirty rags that threaten to tell us who we are and what we are worth, to again see the larger story—the one that reminds us of our Heavenly Father's love, no matter what is happening to us. This is the healthy, grown-up alternative to pretending. But it's not always easy. If you dare to talk about facing life more squarely and honestly, you'll probably get criticism. Even in the church, people may not be interested in hearing about your life as it really is. It may be too threatening, too uncomfortable for them to dare to consider how God might really enter into the ugliest chapters of your life story.

BEAUTY FOR ASHES

> *People wonder why the novel is the most popular form of literature; people wonder why it is read more than books of science or books {on spirituality}. The reason is very simple; it is merely that the novel is more true than they are. Our existence may cease to be a song; it may cease even to be a beautiful lament . . . but our existence is still a story.*[3]
>
> G. K. Chesterton

As a therapist, my experience is teaching me that nothing else keeps a woman in bondage to shame, robbing her of any thought of being a little princess in the eyes of God, more than the incidence of sexual abuse during childhood. Current research shows that one in four women is sexually abused in some way before the age of eight-een, and this is thought by most authorities to be a conservative esti-mate.[4] If you did not experience this kind of abuse during your child-hood, give thanks to God. But you may have experienced other

> *It is a story. Everything's a story. You are a story—I am a story. Miss Minchin is a story.*
>
> *Sarah Crewe*

tragedies that led to similar struggles in your life or relationships.

Unfortunately, those of us in the Christian community sometimes respond to abused women who have crushed spirits with a lack of sensitivity, glibly demanding they "just forgive and get over it" or "put it behind them." Survivors of sexual abuse say that this is not how healing happens. In fact, this attitude can actually encourage women to hang onto unhealthy habits like pretending.

A few years ago, an attractive woman in her mid-forties came to counseling for treatment of major depression. Donna married late in life, around age thirty-five, and had no children. In discussing her physical relationship with her husband, I learned there had been no sexual intimacy for the past two years of their ten-year marriage, although Donna and her husband had been sexually active before marriage. When I questioned her about any possible abuse in her past, she denied it.

"No, I have never been sexually abused," Donna would say. Until one day she let it slip that she did have some memories of exploitation of her body as a young girl.

"I—I didn't want to talk about it," Donna said, trying to choke back tears. "I didn't even want to think about it. I just wanted to pretend it never happened."

As Donna continued in therapy, she began to see that pretending her abuse hadn't occurred wasn't really resolving anything, as proven by her inability to enter into a sexual relationship with her husband. She began the hard work of trying to put together the reality of her abuse with the reality of a loving Heavenly Father who would allow it to happen.

Dr. Diane Langberg, noted Christian counselor and author of *On the Threshold of Hope,* likens this struggle to merge two separate realities to that of victims of Auschwitz who tried to grasp the reality of God with the reality of Auschwitz. God is good and loving / God let my abuse happen. The mind can "short-circuit" when presented with such a challenge.[5]

I proceeded slowly, cautiously, with respect for Donna's tender feelings and confused thoughts. It was not my job to force her to remember things, but to be with her as she recollected the pain of her past and to talk about what really happened. "I believe God does somehow offer me beauty for the ashes of my past," Donna said one day, making reference to a biblical application to her life. "But how? *How* do I take His beauty in exchange for my ashes? What does that mean?"

Good questions. Hard questions. *How can I ever become something beautiful, in light of my past, when I feel so used—like a heap of garbage?* Sara Crewe can point us in the right direction as we ponder such dilemmas. She also found it hard to believe she was a little princess during the hard times. These were Sara's words: *"It would be easy to be a princess if I were dressed in cloth of gold, but it is a great deal more of a triumph to be one all the time."*

In the church, it would be so helpful if we could discuss ways of "fleshing out" how God exchanges His beauty for our ashes. We need to hear other people's stories, so we can see we're not the only ones wrestling with hard questions. Instead, we are often so frozen in fear that we only say things that sound good and right, but have little real meaning to us and offer only a dim reflection of hope to the suffering.

I once heard Joni Eareckson Tada, nationally known author and speaker, share a story that addressed some hard questions when there were no answers to be found. It was a story of a time when she remembered she was a little princess, God's own little princess, even when her paralyzed body threatened to define her as a tattered quadriplegic.

One evening shortly after the accident that caused Joni's paralysis at age seventeen, as she lay motionless on her hospital bed, her best friend on the girls varsity hockey team, Jackie, sneaked into the ward after visiting hours and crawled into her bed. "Jackie!" Joni whispered. "You'll be kicked out of here if they catch you!"

"Shhhh!" was Jackie's only response. Then, with a comforting smile, Jackie laid her head down right next to Joni's and began lovingly stroking her friend's golden hair. As the two girls lay in the bed side by side, faces no more than two inches apart, Jackie began to sing—very softly so that the nurses would not hear: *"Man of Sorrows, what a name, for the Son of God who came, Ruined sinners to reclaim, Hallelujah—What a Savior!"* Jackie sang the song through a couple of times, then, without another word, slipped out of the bed and tiptoed back down the hall.

> *For I know the plans I have for you, declares the Lord, plans to prosper you and not to harm you, plans to give you a hope and a future.*
>
> Jeremiah 29:11

Jackie was attempting to help her friend come to grips with her own Auschwitz. Two realities existed for Joni: God loves me / God let this paralyzing accident happen to me. Joni's life seemed hopeless. She could find no silver lining in the clouds hovering over her. There was no bright side to her reality. Pretending didn't work.

Jackie had no answers to the many questions that must have loomed in Joni's mind. She simply wanted to remind Joni of the Heavenly Father they both belonged to, the One who called them His princesses whether they were clad in cloth of gold or tattered hospital gowns. With tenderness and deep sensitivity, Jackie helped restore Joni's hope by pointing her friend back to Jesus, the Hero of the larger story, who came to reclaim ruined sinners, paralyzed bodies, and broken spirits.

Hallelujah! What a Savior!

After many months of therapy, Donna also began to see that in spite of her painful past, her future was filled with hope. It didn't happen quickly, because she "forgave and forgot," as some well-meaning friends had instructed her. Rather, as we honestly discussed the two realities she lived with, weeks passed. Painful memories would always be a part of Donna's mind, but they became less threatening. Her traumatized mind became calmer as Donna began to accept the realities of her life. She began to see that even though she would probably never understand why God had allowed the abuse, she had always been precious to Him—a little princess. This was truth—the kind of truth that set her free to begin expressing love to her husband in many ways.

w i s d o m   o f   o l d

There's a story in the Bible about a man who lost things dear to him, as some of us have lost things dear to us. He was rejected by his family, abandoned, nearly killed, and left for dead. You're familiar with the story. Joseph's brothers sold him to the Ishmaelites. He was bought by a man named Potiphar, who made Joseph his overseer. That is, until Potiphar's wife accused Joseph of attempting to rape her. As punishment for the crime he was falsely accused of, Joseph was sent to prison. Even after all of that, when Joseph's brothers came to him and asked forgiveness for selling him into slavery in Egypt, here's how Joseph responded: *"But as for you, you meant evil against me, but God meant it for good, in order to bring it about as it is this day, to save many people alive"* (Genesis 50:20, NKJV).

Do you think Joseph might have become discouraged or downhearted at any point? I can't imagine any human being who wouldn't. Even so, years later, one thing had endured. Through it all, Joseph never lost hope, because he remembered he was a member of the royal lineage—he belonged to God. Though he did not always understand what was happening to him,

> *Everything can be taken from a man but one thing: the last of the human freedoms—to choose one's attitude in any given set of circumstances.*[6]
>
> *Viktor Frankl*

Joseph held fast to the Hero of the larger story, refusing to let life's circumstances define him as a slave or a prisoner.

What has caused you to lose hope along your way to becoming a woman? Perhaps you lost a husband? A child? Maybe you lost your childhood innocence due to sexual abuse? No matter what kind of rags and tatters you've had to wear in this life, you must not let shame, past mistakes, poor choices, or any other circumstances be the basis of your hope. With Christ in your heart, you are His little princess. Nothing—absolutely nothing—can change that.

Some days it's easy to remember we're His little princesses, when life dresses us in cloth of gold. But as Sara Crewe has shown us, it's a great deal more of a triumph to remember we're princesses all the time.

God loves us more than we can possibly imagine, beyond all the tattered rags this world may dress us in. If we could be with Him today, we would see it in His eyes. We would hear it in His voice. We would know that even though we don't understand the plot of the story He's writing through our lives, *He does.*

This is why we have hope—because of the *real* story, a true story of rags to riches.

And you are His little princess.

Because your Heavenly Father, the King Himself, the Hero of the larger story, has declared it so.

chapter three

 GRACE

"You ran away from God,

and you can go back."

Heidi

Heidi

by Johanna Spyri

hen Heidi was one year old her mother and father died, and she had to go and live with her Aunt Dete. But Dete and Heidi were not very close, so after four years Dete decided to take Heidi to live with her grandfather in the Swiss Alps. The people in the town nearby thought of the grandfather as a growling, wild man who would not speak to a soul. Some said the death of Heidi's parents was a punishment the grandfather deserved for the godless life he led. But Heidi liked the old man right away, and was not afraid of him. After Dete left Heidi alone with the grandfather, she gazed up at him with a curious look.

"What is it you want?" he bellowed.

"I want to see what you have inside the house." Heidi quickly made herself at home with the grandfather, making a bed in the loft, helping the old man with chores, and talking to the goats. Heidi loved her new home in the mountains with Grandfather. Before long, her merry singing began to lighten his hardened heart. Heidi became a source of pleasure to the grandfather as she followed him step by step in all that he did. She also met Peter, a neighbor boy who tended goats, and his blind grandmother, whom Heidi grew to love. Heidi showed many kindnesses to the grandmother. She wished she could tell a story to the old woman, but Heidi could not read.

When Heidi was seven years old, Aunt Dete returned to take her to live with a wealthy family in Frankfurt and serve as a paid companion to their invalid child, Clara. Heidi loved her mountain home with Grandfather, and she would never have agreed to leave, but Dete tricked her. She promised Heidi she could return home the very next day, bringing fresh white rolls to the blind grandmother. Under this guise, Heidi agreed to go to Frankfurt to visit the family.

How devastating it was when Heidi discovered she was expected to stay with Clara permanently. Although her affection for Clara grew each day, she longed to return to her grandfather. Once she tried to run away and find her way back home. Days and months passed. Heidi met a new grandmother who taught her to read, but her longing to return home only grew stronger. She became thin and pale, and thought perhaps the people she loved and wanted to see again had died. She no longer smiled or sang. Finally, a doctor determined that Heidi was consumed with homesickness and must be allowed to go home.

On the day she was taken back to the mountain, her heart beat faster, and she was so overflowing with joy and thankfulness that she could only shout, "Grandfather! Grandfather! Grandfather!" A happy reunion followed, as Heidi greeted the blind grandmother, Peter, and her goat friends. The wealthy family had given Heidi money, and she spent some of it to bring fresh rolls to the grandmother. Now that she could read, Heidi often read hymns to the grandmother, which pleased the old woman greatly.

One day as Heidi was skipping along holding her grandfather's hand, she told the old man that during her days away in Frankfurt, she had prayed to return home to him quickly. When it didn't happen, she was deeply grieved, thinking God must not care about her wishes, so she gave up praying. "But now I am glad that God did not let me have at once all I prayed and wept for!" she exclaimed. She realized that during the days of waiting, she'd earned money to buy the grandmother fresh bread, and she'd also learned to read. "So we will pray every day, won't we, Grandfather, and never forget Him again."

The grandfather, however, who had not always lived virtuously, believed God had forgotten all about him years ago. He answered, sadly, "And if once it is so, it is so always; no one can go back, and he whom God has forgotten, is forgotten forever."

"Oh, no, Grandfather, we can go back. . . . I will read it to you and you will see how beautiful it is." Then Heidi sat down with the old man, remembering the time when she herself had turned away from God, thinking He didn't care about her. She read the story of the Prodigal Son to the grandfather, finishing by saying that when the father saw his son returning, he had compassion and ran, and fell on his neck and kissed him.

"You are right, Heidi, it is a beautiful tale," said the grandfather, but he looked so grave that Heidi grew silent. That night after Heidi went to sleep, the grandfather climbed up the ladder to the loft and put his lamp down near her bed. He stood a long time gazing down at her without speaking. At last, he folded his hands and bowed his head and said in a low voice, "Father, I have sinned against heaven and before Thee and am not worthy to be called Thy son." And two large tears rolled down the old man's cheeks.

The next morning the grandfather called up to Heidi, "Come along,

Heidi! The sun is up! Put on your best frock for we are going to church together!" The townspeople were happy to see Heidi and her grandfather, and from that day on, the people knew they had misjudged the crusty old hermit. His gruff exterior was only a disguise for a kindly, yet fearful man.

Heidi lived happily with the grandfather. In the spring, Clara and her family came to the mountain for a long visit. In the fresh air and the warmth of Heidi's friendship, Clara learned to walk. The blind grandmother had fresh rolls to eat every day. "Heidi, read me one of the hymns!" the grandmother requested at the book's end. "I can do nothing for the remainder of my life but thank the Father in heaven for all the mercies He has shown us!"[1]

mentor's wisdom

I somehow skipped over the heartwarming story of *Heidi* during my growing up days, and read the book for the first time as an adult. Quickly baited by the trail of tender truths and familiar themes scattered across the surface of the story, I was enticed to dive in deeper. A child's innocent prayers, friendship with animals, the joy of living in nature, a hardened heart melted by fearless love—these are themes that reach deep into my soul. How about you?

Who else but Heidi could have led a hostile hermit to a place beyond the bondage of his anger and shame, back into the open arms of a loving God? She instantly loved the unlovely grandfather. Aunt Dete was no saint either, taking a vulnerable little girl to the reputedly unsafe home of the grandfather. Though a child Heidi's age would not have been capable of perceiving the more subtle sins of her elders, she was able beyond her years when it came to understanding grace.

OPEN HEART, OPEN ARMS

The two major causes of most emotional problems among evangelical Christians are these: the failure to understand, receive, and live out God's unconditional grace and forgiveness; and the failure to give out that unconditional love, forgiveness, and grace to other people.[2]

David Seamands

Heidi helped the grandfather take steps toward what Dutch priest Henri Nouwen once called "the place where I so much want to be, but am so fearful of being. It is the place where I will receive all I desire, all that I ever hoped for, all that I will ever need, but it is also . . . the place that confronts me with the fact that truly accepting love, forgiveness, and healing is . . . beyond earning, deserving, and rewarding. It is the place of surrender and complete trust."[3]

Stuck in the muck of his own failures and fears, the grandfather had isolated himself and completely lost touch with the flow of giving and receiving love and forgiveness. Ironically, only these simple tidbits of truth Heidi was casting before the old man, one at a time, could nourish his starving soul. It took the grace of a loving child who would invite him to venture away from the shallow shore of self-protectiveness, through the waters of reconciliation, back to the deeper stream of inner peace.

We don't often see people giving such lavish grace to others around them, so when we do come across someone who embodies this quality, even a smidgen of it, we stand up and take notice. Often it's children who are most likely to offer unmerited favor to others. Perhaps they, like Heidi, have not lived long enough to develop the bad habit of holding onto shame and guilt, keeping God at arm's length as the grandfather did for many years.

Sharon, a friend with two small children, recently told me a story about her six-year-old daughter. Little Tara's first-grade class was planning a parent-child talent show. The date was set well in advance, so the parents had plenty of time to practice singing or dancing or reading a poem with their children in preparation for the special day, which would be held on a weekday after school.

On the morning of the talent show, Tara was excited to show all her friends how she and her mommy could sing "The Yellow Rose of Texas" accompanied by an instrumental recording. They planned to wear matching yellow dresses they'd purchased especially for the show. That same morning, one of Sharon's Mary Kay customers called for an "emergency" makeover. Apparently, the woman had been asked to make a television appearance as a fill-in when the regular person came down with the flu.

You can probably guess the rest of the story. Sharon thought surely she could finish the customer's makeup in time to get to her daughter's school. Then, when things took longer than she anticipated, Sharon had to make a choice between leaving the customer halfway made-up to get to the school on time or getting the lady camera-ready, knowing she might arrive too late to participate with her daughter in the talent show. She chose the latter.

Heading across town toward the school, she hit a major traffic pile-up, which only made things worse. When Sharon finally arrived at the school, her daughter was sitting on the front steps waiting. Most of the children had already gone home. "Oh, honey, I'm so sorry," Sharon said, crying and running toward Tara, then hugging her daughter to her chest. "I feel just awful! There was a bad accident, but I might have made it on time if I'd left earlier. Can you ever forgive me?"

Little Tara, all dressed in yellow, looked into her mother's tear-stained face and said, "Don't cry, Mommy. I forgive you."

"What?" asked Sharon. "How can you say that? Aren't you mad at me?" Tara explained to her mom that when it was time for their number and Sharon wasn't there, one of the teachers had asked if Tara wanted to sing her song alone, or skip her turn. "I'll sing by myself," she'd replied.

The audience knew what happened and gave Tara a standing ovation for her courage when her song was over. This, along with a snow cone the teacher gave her, had apparently consoled the little girl. "It's okay, Mommy, really," Tara reassured. Even so, it would take some time for Sharon to give up the shame she felt for letting her daughter down.

Young children often have the ability to forgive quickly, eagerly restoring an adult to the former place of favor following an offense. Also, kids don't appear to get hung up concentrating on their own sins. Perhaps their ability to freely give and receive grace is a part of a child's innocence (relatively speaking, at least). As Heidi recalled the days in Frankfurt when she gave up on God and stopped saying her prayers, she realized she didn't really *deserve* to return to Him with no questions asked. Yet when she was ready to go back to Him, she didn't waste any time worrying about rejection.

By the time we've grown into adults, many of us have lost the freedom to eagerly offer grace to others. Likewise, as we gain life experience, we may have difficulty being on the receiving end of unmerited favor. Like the grandfather, it is difficult for any of us to believe God would actually want us back when we have forsaken Him.

For many years, I would have identified with the grandfather, hanging onto the guilt and shame of my past, believing God was punishing me for my sins. I was convinced He was mad at me, and that's why my life didn't turn out as well as I'd once hoped it would. Sad to say, during the first twenty years of my life as a Christian, I sort of went through the motions of the spiritual life, but in my heart, I held God at arm's length.

When as a middle-aged adult I discovered God's grace, I came to see the truth of the words Heidi shared with the grandfather—the truth of God's unconditional love. This meant His love was mine as a gift, a free gift I could never pay for, or deserve, or perform well enough to earn, or even learn enough about to fully comprehend. Furthermore, at times when I would turn my back on Him throughout my life, God would always be eager for my return. Maybe your heart is also yearning for an understanding of the lavish nature of God's grace.

THE ONE JESUS LOVES

Do you long to respond to God as Heidi did, eagerly returning to Him after you've spent some time away or turned your back on Him? Do you yearn to accept the grace of God? One day, one of my clients who had been coming for counseling several months told me she'd found a way to remind herself every morning that God's love for her is unconditional, and that He always wants to be close to her. As part of her morning worship, she looks in the mirror and gives herself a great big smile, just as she would smile at a friend. Then she turns her face toward heaven and says out loud, "Dear God, today I accept Your love for me! Thank You for always wanting me, no matter what!" How much it must please our Heavenly Father to have His gift received with such childlike joy.

But you are a forgiving God, gracious and compassionate, slow to anger and abounding in love.

Nehemiah 9:17b

In the Gospels, the disciple John is called "the one Jesus loved." At one of Brennan Manning's seminars, he referred to the close relationship between Christ and John, saying, "If John were to be asked, 'What is your primary identity in life?' he would not reply, 'I am a disciple, an apostle, an evangelist, an author of one of the four Gospels,' but rather, 'I am the one Jesus loves.' "[4]

46

wisdom of old

Do you know that *you* are the one Jesus loves? Or do you find yourself holding back from God, turning away from Him because you feel you don't deserve His love anymore? We find accounts of God's unconditional love scattered throughout the Bible, both in the Old Testament and the New Testament. Often, however, and sometimes unaware, we can magnify the part about God's anger when we go away from Him, and think it means He doesn't want us back, or that He is still angry and doesn't love us anymore.

Nestled in the midst of the story of *Heidi,* we come upon the touching scene many of us may need to revisit as adults, when the child tells the grandfather about the grace of God. Sitting next to the old man, with book in hand, Heidi read the story of the prodigal son in Luke 15. When she came to the place in the story where the son wanted to return to the father, Heidi paused and asked the grandfather, "What do you think happens now? Do you think the father is still angry and will say to him 'I told you so!'" The old man sat silently, trance-like, gazing at the pictures in Heidi's book.

Then she pushed the book gently in front of him and said, "See how happy he is there?" pointing with her finger to the returned Prodigal Son, all dressed up in fresh, clean clothes, and standing beside his father. Heidi's story gently reawakened thoughts and feelings the grandfather had long since put to rest.

In the Book of Hosea we find another touching account of God's unconditional love. Hosea's love for Gomer, his unfaithful wife, vividly pictures God's love for Israel, His chosen but unfaithful people. Hosea reveals to us the heart of God. How He suffers when we go away from Him, but He never stops wooing us back, longing for our return.

"My people are determined to turn from me," God said. Then listen to His beautiful heart-cry for the return of His beloved in chapter eleven. *"How can I give you up? How can I hand you over? My heart is changed within me; all my compassion is aroused, and I will not carry out my fierce anger. I will not come in wrath."*

Rend your heart and not your garments. Return to the Lord your God, for he is gracious and compassionate, slow to anger and abounding in love, and he relents from sending calamity.

Joel 2:13

Are you afraid God is mad at you, or is punishing you for your mistakes? In his devotional book *Reflections for Ragamuffins*, Brennan Manning explains why these notions became obsolete with the Advent of Christ, who came for those He loves: sinners.

> *Under the old covenant there is no forgiveness for those who remain sinners: the sinner faces judgment. But the God of Jesus does not judge us, for he loves even those who are evil. In a word, the Father of Jesus loves sinners. He is the only God man has ever heard of who behaves this way. Unreal gods, the inventions of men, despise sinners. But the Father of Jesus loves all, no matter what they do. And this, of course, is almost too incredible for us to accept.*[5]

As Heidi says, "We can go back!" We don't deserve God's love. No matter how hard we try to be good, we can never earn His love. That's what grace is—unmerited favor. It's a gift, especially for those of us who don't deserve it. And no matter how many times we run away, or how far away we go, we can always go back. When we do, we will always find a loving Father with open arms waiting for us, longing with all His heart for our return.

chapter four

FREE SPIRIT

"Isn't this a free country? Can't a person

walk any way she wants to?"

Pippi

Pippi Longstocking
by Astrid Lindgren

Pippi Longstocking was a spunky young girl with a free spirit, who went on one hilarious adventure after another. The picture on the cover of my paperback version depicts her winsome ways better than any words can. With smiling, freckled face upturned toward the sun, eyes closed in delight, red braids sticking straight out, Pippi flings her arms wide as if to embrace the world.

Next door to two friends named Tommy and Annika, Pippi lived in a house called Villa Villekulla with a pet monkey and a horse as her only companions. Pippi's mother was in heaven, and her father was a sea captain who disappeared after being blown overboard from his ship in a storm. She was absolutely certain, however, that her father would return someday.

Meanwhile, the spontaneous young girl found ways to turn every-day household chores into bold adventures. For example, Pippi's way of cleaning a floor was to strap scrub brushes onto the bottoms of her shoes and "skate" across the surface. (It took a lot of suds to scrub sugary dough off the linoleum after she'd rolled and cut cookies on the floor!) But nothing was more fun for Pippi than a party.

One day Tommy and Annika's mother invited a few ladies to a coffee party, and Pippi was asked to come too. The overjoyed girl dressed in her most stylish clothes for this special occasion. Although she had no training in social graces, Pippi was determined to take part in the coffee table talk, whether she knew anything about the subject or not! When the hostess asked whether Pippi would prefer one lump of sugar or two, Pippi quickly asserted she'd rather have "five lumps, thank you."

After making a series of social flubs, Pippi was sent home. "Forgive me because I couldn't behave myself!" she called over her shoulder as she departed. Though Pippi had always been secretly afraid she could not behave properly around adults (and now she'd proven it), she was not about to let a little fear of future failure ruin her life.

Pippi Longstocking's free spirit sometimes takes grown-ups a while to understand, though all children absolutely love her. But by story's end, Pippi is sure to win the favor of readers of all ages. [1]

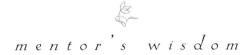

mentor's wisdom

£ive as if you were living a second time, and as though you had acted wrongly the first time. [2]

Viktor Frankl

What an impudent child! Completely unaware of social etiquette. No doubt these were the thoughts of the ladies at the coffee party Pippi attended.

But the criticism of adults didn't faze Pippi. She was lost in her own world of adventure, on the lookout for fun ways to get through the trials and difficulties of everyday life. With a knack for breaking tradition and no parents around to supervise, Pippi had little regard for manners and etiquette.

She's a character who gets under the skin of those who prefer the prim and proper to the joys of spontaneity. But if we take a closer look at her approach to life, I believe we can learn a lot about living in the freedom Christ has provided for us as His children. Somewhere along the way as we try to live out our faith in God, we can get off track, concentrating our efforts on proper procedures, always doing our spiritual chores in the same ways. I don't know if this has ever happened to you, but it has certainly been a part of my experience.

By the dawn of adulthood, most of us have learned the laws of society and take pride in our ability to keep them. Around ten years of age, however, girls are at the pinnacle of their free, childlike, creative selves, before puberty begins to conform them to the images seen in the media. Pippi is this quintessential little girl. Though rules have their place, when it comes to living a joyful life in bold freedom, Pippi has a lot to teach us. She was not afraid to try new things, take risks, or break tradition.

How about you? Do you ever do things differently from the way they've always been done? Sometimes change is sorely needed, even in such matters as longstanding family holiday traditions. But it's not always easy to initiate such changes. If you try it, you might as well expect to get a little criticism.

A friend named Nancy dreaded the hectic pace of the holiday season. The pumpkins and goblins hadn't even made it to the store display shelves yet, and Nancy was already dreading Christmas. "The minute our feet hit the floor on Christmas morning, we shift into high gear, house-hopping from Grandma's to Aunt Bea's to Cousin David's," she said one day as we shared lunch. Her tension was visible. "Then we finally arrive back at our house on overload just in time to fall back into our beds. It's awful!"

How sad, I thought, as I listened to her tale of tension, *that the birthday of our Savior should be celebrated in such a way. Yet what a common experience this is, especially among young families.* As the holidays drew nearer, Nancy and I discussed possibilities that might be somewhat less traditional, yet provide their family a little more "peace on earth."

"I've got an idea," Nancy said. "I don't know if my husband will go for this or not, and it would really be different, but I'd absolutely love to just get up and take things a lot more slowly." Nancy had several ideas to present to her husband and elementary school-aged daughters. The following week, she excitedly detailed a new tradition her family of four had decided to try.

"On Christmas morning after opening our presents, everyone stayed in their pajamas and enjoyed a leisurely breakfast of cinnamon rolls from a neighborhood bakery, served on our best china, just for a touch of fun. The girls loved the contrast between our fanciest dishes and their comfy flannel pjs. The entire morning was relaxing, enjoyable, even a bit magical."

These are pretty drastic changes, I thought to myself. But from Nancy's previous description of their family's holiday chaos, it was time to try doing some things differently to restore some sense of sacredness to the celebration of Christ's birth.

"Around noon, we got dressed," Nancy continued, obviously overjoyed with this new, creative holiday approach. "Then we went to Aunt Jane's, since it was her turn to host the family dinner this year. *One* trip"—Nancy paused for emphasis, holding up an index finger—"to *one* house. The girls told all our relatives what a fun time we had at our 'pajama breakfast.' Even though their aunts and uncles were angry for the first hour or so after we arrived, before the day was over, some of them actually said they might try our new idea themselves!"

This is the sense of bold adventure we see in Pippi Longstocking—finding freedom to take risks and make changes when they will create a better life. In Pippi's own words, *"Isn't this a free country? Can't a person walk any way she wants to?"* Breaking family holiday traditions is not always desirable. Even when it is, change may not go over well. But for Nancy and her clan, a touch of holiday simplicity helped turn Christmas back into a holy day.

PLAYING LIFE BY EAR

To discover movements of freedom in oneself where there has been only fear-ridden and cowering subjection . . . {this is} gloriously worth doing.[3]

Eugene Peterson

Pippi learned early on that failure was a part of life, and that some things like friends and cheerfulness were more important than rules. (I bet she even colored outside the lines when she was very small.) This is a lesson that took me about forty years to learn. But my sister, Jan, has always had a lot in common with Pippi. Jan and I are planning to meet each other soon in San Francisco with our husbands and do the town up right. Maybe catch *Phantom of the Opera* at the San Francisco Playhouse, walk up and down the steep, twisted cobblestone streets, and eat fish and chips on Fisherman's Wharf. We're sisters and close friends now, but it hasn't always been that way.

Growing up, Jan played life by ear, while I tried hard to keep the rules. She was two years older than I, so her weekly allowance was a bit more than mine. As I recall, by the time she was in high school, she got five dollars a week. I only got three dollars, but that was not bad for a seventh grader. I'd save up for weeks at a time while she squandered her money on nail polish and 45 rpm records. On any given day, I'd have more cash in my money jar than she'd have. Can you guess which one of us made her bed first thing every morning, and who only made hers on weekends? "It's not fair," I'd whine, when Mother occasionally bought extra things for Jan—things I thought she should have saved up her *own* money for.

Are you getting the idea I was just a bit judgmental? Perhaps not unlike a small version of one of the ladies at the coffee party? Well, okay, I admit it. Just as the stuffy ladies were intolerant when Pippi interrupted them or spoke with her mouth full, I couldn't stand it when Jan got by with breaking our parents' rules. I worked hard to abide by them, and I expected plenty of praise and recognition for my efforts.

But when it came to trying new things, or having fun, interesting experiences, Jan ran way ahead of me. Whether it was getting up the nerve to jump off the roof into our daddy's arms, competing with the neighborhood boys in a game of baseball, or running for elementary student body president, Jan was game for a new adventure.

Who has modeled this kind of free spirit for you? Who is your Pippi Longstocking? She will be someone who is not afraid to try new things, who doesn't always conform, and who cares more about the adventures of life than strictly adhering to traditions, rituals, and the usual way of doing things. Even though we've grown into women, someone with a childlike spirit may come to mind.

A lot of years have passed since my sister and I shared our childhood. During adolescence, competition and envy took their toll. I moved to Texas, she stayed in northern California. Many things changed. But Jan's free spirit endured over time, while mine withered beneath an overzealous commitment to do what was expected, often at the expense of genuine, healthy self-expression.

Jan came to visit me about a year and a half ago. It was the first time since our mom died, and now we're all each other has left of our family of origin. It was November, and the trees were bright orange and yellow. I felt proud of Texas. Jan and I had fun cooking dinners together, and I showed her around my southern section of the world. But my favorite part of our visit was late at night when our husbands had gone to bed and we stayed up late eating leftover pizza, talking until two or three in the morning. We had a lot to talk over, things we couldn't say to each other when we were girls.

The most cherished moment of the entire visit was during one of those late-night conversations, this one about our regrets that we hadn't kept closer tabs on each other through the years. We were sitting at the kitchen table when Jan leaned forward as if to give me a hug. But instead, she smiled broadly and stood up, asking me to stand and face her. With noses nearly touching, Jan looked deeply, even dramatically, into my eyes. Then she began speaking slowly, "Now just let me look at you. You're my little sister. My only sister."

When she paused to clear her throat, I took a mental snapshot of this Kodak Moment to savor for years to come. Her eyes, now moist with tears, sparkled like hypnotic pools. I was mesmerized by the joy of that instant, wondering what was coming next, as she went on to say, "I want you to know I am so-o-o proud of you." It was as if the whole world stood up and cheered for me, but her voice was the only one I could hear.

"Oh, Jan! Oh, sister," I said, crying softy, laying my head on her chest. "Thank you." It was that same Pippi Longstocking spirit she'd always had, now showing up in a different, more mature way. For sisters in a conservative clan that traditionally showed little emotion (let alone pronounced a heartfelt blessing on other family members), it was a bit risky to make such a bold statement of love. We'd never been very close or spent a lot of time together. But she'd dared to tear down a long-standing wall of sibling rivalry that stood between us, and as she did, some of her liberating love spilled over onto me. That evening, Jan and I began to care for each other in a new way—in mutual, joyous freedom.

FREE SPOT

When I was growing up, my aunts, uncles, and cousins seldom got together because most of our relatives lived in another state. But when our extended family did have a reunion, we'd often push back from the dinner table and settle in for a leisurely afternoon playing Bingo.

"B-9, I-23, Free Spot, G-54, O-71!" I called out my numbers to verify that I, a twelve-year-old, had just won the first round. Then I cleared my game card, eager to see if I could win two in a row. Placing my first token on the middle square of the Bingo card (marked "Free Spot"), I was all set.

> *Paradoxically it is the acceptance of God that makes you free and delivers you from human tyranny.*[4]
>
> Thomas Merton,
> New Seeds of Contemplation

In the game of Bingo, everyone gets a "free spot"—sort of like the space of pardon God provides for His children, so we don't have to carry the burden of guilt for our sins. If you are a woman like me, who tried hard to keep all the rules, but no matter how hard you tried still messed up somewhere along the way, it may be difficult to live in the "free spot" God has given you. You may have spent a lot of time and effort trying to adhere to overly rigid structures and self-imposed religious confinement. If so, it may be time to adjust your expectations. Because that's precisely what they are—your expectations, not God's.

We will all blow it in one way or another, without even trying. There's no question about that. Here again, we can take a lesson from Pippi. When she messed up by interrupting others or talking too much at the coffee party, and was finally asked to leave, she didn't waste a lot time feeling burdened by false guilt. (Remember that she had no adults to teach her about social graces.) She simply said, "Forgive me because I couldn't behave myself!" The amazing part is that even though we don't always behave ourselves either, God generously forgives, and offers *a free spot*—His grace—in the midst of a guilt-ridden world.

He wants us to embrace life in the *free spot* created by Christ's death on our behalf. God knows we won't have all our tokens lined up in a row with no gaps. He doesn't expect more of us than we can deliver. Our parents may, and our coworkers or husbands may. But God accepts us and keeps on loving us, even though things in our lives don't line up in perfect rows.

Have you ever felt guilty because you missed church or skipped your morning prayer time? Maybe you spent a Sunday morning relaxing in your backyard, taking in the wonder of God's creation instead of attending your usual worship service. Or you got out of bed a half-hour after your alarm went off, so your feet hit the floor running; then later, you found yourself avoiding God because you'd "let Him down." Sometimes we get so socked into our spiritual routines that a little flexibility or spontaneity seems like a sin. Do you really think God keeps a Sunday School attendance chart, or cares whether we pray at six in the morning, two in the afternoon, or at midnight?

God isn't concerned with rigid structures. He wants us to come to Him because He loves us, and wants to remind us that He's right there with us, no matter what. I think our Heavenly Father would be delighted with Pippi's attitude when it comes to the spiritual life. She helps us learn that God wants us to walk in freedom, living out our uniquely designed lives with childlike joy.

The free space of liberty God grants us is not given as a license to sin wildly, but as an invitation to trade in our guilt for gratitude. What a privilege it is to be able to choose the time of day I like best for prayer, Bible reading, or singing to the Lord. How wonderful it is to have freedom to be creative in personal worship, to do a praise dance if I'm inspired to, to read a dramatic psalm on my front porch with Mozart playing in the background if the mood strikes, or to have a prayer time by candlelight if I'm feeling especially meditative or melancholy. When it comes to our life with God, we really do live in a "free country"—the free spot of God's grace.

wisdom of old

Like my sister and me, Martha and Mary of Bethany (sisters of Lazarus, in Luke 10:38-42), were quite different from each other. Jesus loved them both. Martha was a hard worker who did things by the book. (She probably made her bed every morning too.) Mary took advantage of opportunities as they came along. In this passage, she sat at the feet of Jesus, listening to what He said.

Martha became frustrated because Mary wasn't helping with the cooking and serving. The way managerial Martha saw things, Mary was loafing, getting out of all the work. "Lord, don't You care that my sister has left me to do the work by myself? Tell her to help me!" Poor Martha. I can relate to her—wanting to be noticed, trying so hard to keep all the rules and do everything efficiently, even attempting to manipulate Jesus. She must have been shocked with His response:

"Martha, Martha, you are worried and upset about many things, but only one thing is needed. Mary has chosen what is better, and it will not be taken away from her." Mary didn't want to miss this opportunity to sit with Jesus, anointing Him with fragrant oil, and wiping His feet with her hair (John 11:2). Lost in an adventure with her Lord, Mary shows us a quiet way of living in freedom.

When we think of people with free spirits, most often the "life of the party" types come to mind, people who make us laugh, those who end up at the center of attention. But you don't have to be loud, boisterous, or humorous to have a free spirit. You may be a quiet, gentler type like Mary, who enjoys the present moment, free to follow a different routine in a spirit of serendipity at times, even though it may bring you criticism.

Like Mary of Bethany, Pippi Longstocking also had her quiet, reflective moments. This was another side of her free spirit. Although Pippi made the best of her life without her parents, sometimes she sorely missed them. When she felt sad and alone, she sometimes had imaginary conversations with her mother (who had long since died). And Pippi talked often of her father's anticipated return.

Just as Pippi missed her father, we also look forward to being with our Father someday. When we join Him in heaven, we will be completely free. Until that day, let us not become enslaved again to rules, laden with guilt, preoccupied with our sins. Let us be more like our freckle-faced friend with the stick-out braids—alive in the present moment, free to risk, to try new things, aware of our freedom in Christ. We owe her a debt of gratitude for her spunky storybook reminder, so I'll end this chapter with a fitting tribute to our mentor's spirit: Three cheers for Pippi Longstocking!

> *It is for freedom that Christ has set us free. Stand firm, then, and do not let yourselves be burdened again by a yoke of slavery.*
>
> Galatians 5:1

chapter five

OPTIMISM

"When you're hunting for the glad things, you sort of forget the other kind."

Pollyanna

Pollyanna

b y   E l e a n o r   H .   P o r t e r

Miss Polly Harrington, a wealthy woman with a cold disposition, was alarmed when she received a telegram saying her niece, Pollyanna Whittier, needed a guardian after her father's death. Polly's estranged brother, a poor minister, was Pollyanna's father, and since there were no other relatives to take the child in, Polly reluctantly agreed to let her newly orphaned niece stay in the cold, musty attic room of her mansion.

Despite Aunt Polly's grouchy disposition, Pollyanna played a game her father taught her before he died, the "just being glad" game. No matter what happened, Pollyanna tried to find something to be happy about. Motivated by an underlying sense of goodness, Pollyanna helped with charity projects for the Ladies Aid Society. She filled her days with good deeds, seeing past frowns and scowls on people's faces, right down into their hearts. Pollyanna's world was full of problems, to be sure, but one by one they were resolved. In time, the Glad Girl helped the entire town look on the brighter side. Even the embittered local preacher, Reverend Ford, changed

> *They are never alone who are accompanied by joyful thoughts.*[1]
>
> Sir Philip Sydney

his lifelong "fire and brimstone" sermons and began to focus on "rejoicing texts."

Then one day Pollyanna was hit by a car and paralyzed. Though it was a challenge to find anything positive about being crippled, Pollyanna managed to find something—for she had at last won her aunt's affection.

"And so it's *hurt* that I am, and not sick," said Pollyanna, as Aunt Polly perched on the side of her bed, after the accident. "Well, I'm glad of that."

"G-glad, Pollyanna?"

"Yes. Broken legs get well," Pollyanna responded. "I'm glad it isn't smallpox that ails me too."

"You seem to—to be glad for a good many things, my dear," said Aunt Polly, with great affection.

"I am . . . I'm glad of some things I haven't said yet. I don't know but I'm 'most glad I was hurt."

"Pollyanna!" exclaimed Aunt Polly.

"Well, you see, since I have been hurt, you've called me 'dear' lots of times and you didn't before. . . . When you're hunting for the glad things, you sort of forget the other kind."

Aunt Polly did not answer, but her eyes were filled with tears. Finally even she was convinced that there's something good in every situation. She was reunited with the boyfriend of her youth, the town doctor, whom she had always secretly loved. Pollyanna was then taken to a specialist who eventually helped her walk again.[2]

m e n t o r ' s   w i s d o m

It had been a long time since I'd read the story of Pollyanna. I'd long ago (probably by about age twelve) adopted a cynical attitude toward this look-on-the-bright-side-no-matter-what girl, and others like her. Being glad in the midst of poverty, orphanhood, and undeserved suffering. Barf. How disgusting. Or so I thought at twelve years of age.

How about you? What comes to mind when you think of Pollyanna? Do you envision a ditzy blonde with a pasted-on smile, floating along blithely in her apple-pie world? Someone who's all sweetness-and-light, responding to life with calculated, predictable joy, come what may? Insert success, out comes joy. Insert failure, out comes joy. Insert loss, out comes joy. This is how I've thought of Pollyanna all these years. But after recently rereading this classic story, I see I've given Pollyanna a bad rap.

As a woman, I find her a warm, caring, genuine girl who filled her time doing good deeds for others in spite of her personal hardships. I am drawn to her, as I am to many women whose optimism balances out my tendency to worry and fret about life (what if . . . the worst thing happens?). These positive and truthful thinkers are not pretending, at least not for the most part. (Remember, as we talked about in the chapter on *A Little Princess*, we all pretend at times, even without trying.) But in this chapter, we're considering those few people who naturally focus on the optimistic side, calmly expecting the best from life.

THINKING OPTIMISTICALLY AND TRUTHFULLY

Pollyanna viewed life through the dual lenses of optimism and truthfulness.

As the story opens, her father had just passed away. Life was beginning to wear this eleven-year-old girl down when she came to live with Aunt Polly, someone she didn't know very well. Yet Pollyanna did not hide her tears or sadness when she missed her father. On those rare occasions when she felt despondent, everybody around her knew it. At the end of the story, when it looked like she might never walk again, Pollyanna did not plaster on a plastic smile with no regard for the world around her.

For an eleven-year-old girl, Pollyanna was not a phony. (I think that is what really gets under our skin, rather than a positive, upbeat attitude.) Her reactions to life and people were optimistic, yet very human. The foundation for Pollyanna's ability to think positively and truthfully seems to be her underlying sense of goodness, which motivated her to get

> *Since we cannot change reality, let us change the eyes which see reality.*[3]
>
> Niko Kazantzakis

involved in charity projects, visit the sick, and bring joy to others. She saw past frowns and scowls on people's faces, deep down into their hearts. Her fascination for the small joys of life spilled over like a freshly drawn bubble bath overflowing onto the outlooks of others.

Author and speaker Lindsey O'Connor tells how her young daughter helped her develop a more optimistic attitude during the dark days following Lindsey's beloved mother's death. Understandably, Lindsey was grief-stricken. In one fell swoop she'd lost her mother and her best friend to cancer. Some months had gone by, and Lindsey was still crying more than she wanted to, feeling stuck in her healing.

Then one day she walked out into the yard where her little girl was picking dandelions.

"Look, Mommy!" her daughter called. "See the pretty flower?"

"That's not a flower, it's a weed," Lindsey said absentmindedly. "Put that down."

"No, Mommy, it's a flower! See?" The child raised the puffball before her face as she took in a deep breath and blew the wispy fluff from the stalk. "See?" she repeated. "It is a flower!"

In that instant, Lindsey was called back to the present moment to share a glimpse of joy with her daughter. A four year old had just reminded her mother that she had a choice about how she viewed her circumstances. She could not change the reality of her loss. But she could choose to set her mind on the positive side. She could decide to cherish the good memories of her mom and celebrate the closeness they shared for years. This is a classic case of reality-based optimism: taking time to come to acceptance of loss, then focusing on the good gifts we have today.

But what happens if we try to think optimistically, yet without respect for truth? This is what I did for several years before my first marriage ended. My husband and I weren't communicating. He was withdrawn, preoccupied with his work, depressed. Yet I carried on with a cheery "rejoice and be glad" attitude, glibly ignoring our problems, distracting myself with a phony religious preoccupation. Why? Because I thought it was the right thing to do, the optimistic attitude I should have as a Christian.

All the while, unbeknownst to me, my husband was involved in an affair, spending more and more time "at the office." I was afraid to confront truth, and I suppose my husband was, too. Eventually, there was a huge price to pay—divorce—partly because I tried to be optimistic with no regard for the truth of our circumstances. When a person disregards truth, reality is compromised and one's witness loses credibility. Adventures in "La-la Land" can't last forever.

Did Pollyanna have this same problem? I don't think so. For an eleven year old, she actually had quite a lot of emotional integrity.

PORTRAIT OF A GLAD GIRL

> *In the midst of winter, I finally learned that there was in me an invincible summer.*[4]
>
> **Albert Camus**

Assuming she grew up to become a mature woman, what do you think

Pollyanna would look like today? Does someone come to mind, perhaps a mentor who has that same optimistic spirit, whose heart is overflowing with goodness?

I can't help but think of my sister-in-law, Karen. A colorful sanguine (down to her hot pink sneakers) in terms of Florence Littauer's "Personality Tree," Karen is an outgoing woman, concerned for the well-being of others. Her warm, contagious smile attracts people of all ages, and her positive approach to life evokes my deepest admiration. (Come to think of it, Karen even has the blonde Pollyanna-like braids, though they're a bit shorter than our classic Glad Girl's.)

Like Pollyanna, Karen has had her share of bumps and scrapes. When my husband, Frank, and his two sisters were small children, their mother died suddenly. Karen was ten years old at the time. I've often thought how difficult it must have been for the three of them to lose their mother, move to a new home in another town, and adjust to a new step-mom, all within one year. Whew! What an emotional load for each of them. Of course, I didn't know Karen back then, but I imagine that even as a youngster, she managed to find a little cheer in the midst of loss and adjustments.

I first met Karen when the Waggoner clan got together shortly after Frank and I were married. "Welcome to the family," she said, with arms open wide. "I feel as though I already know you because Frank has talked about you so much." She gave me a radiant, welcoming smile. "And I know you've gotta be topnotch, or my brother wouldn't have picked you!"

Several years later, Karen's husband, Mike, died suddenly of a heart attack after over twenty years of life together. The tragic news was a shock, since he was only in his late fifties. "I don't know how I'll live without Mike," Karen said, when Frank and I phoned her just after we'd gotten the news. "Somehow God will get me through all of this."

Karen continued to grieve, as anyone would after the loss of a husband. "I'm surviving, one day at a time," she'd often say into the telephone receiver, beginning our frequent phone chats. "My friends here are being so supportive. You wouldn't believe all the great food they're bringing in."

At times Karen even joked around, making light of her dire situation. "How about you find me a rich Texan? I'm all alone and I need a man!" But she never used humor to avoid truth. It just helped to be less serious once in a while.

Then Karen came to visit us in Texas. When her youngest daughter graduated from high school and went away to college, Karen knew she could use a little extra family support. While I sincerely believed Frank and I could encourage her during our visit, by the time Karen left to return to her home in the Boston area, I knew for sure we were the beneficiaries. Her positive, hopeful spirit, balanced with a heart of integrity, filled our home with joy. We cried together, and we even laughed a little. We planted flowers, gathered vegetables from our garden, cooked good meals, introduced her to many of our friends (they all loved her), and stayed up until midnight talking and reminiscing.

"Oh, I've had such a wonderful time here. Now it's your turn to come and visit me real soon," Karen coaxed. "I want to take you moonlight canoeing! Did I tell you that's my new favorite pastime?"

"Uhhh, moonlight canoeing?" Frank stammered. I wondered if he was as amazed as I was that Karen could think of sporting adventures so soon after her husband's death. I admit my analytical mind went to work, trying to identify any defense mechanisms or denial tactics she might be using. "Well, no," Frank replied. "I've never even canoed much in the daytime, Karen."

"Well, you haven't lived till you've seen the rippling lake water shimmering underneath a midnight sky. I guess it's my grief therapy." Karen's voice took on a more somber tone. For a moment, her eyes glazed over, as

69

if staring into some faraway place unknown to me. We just sat silently, waiting. It was a moment of sacredness, as Frank and I could guess what Karen was thinking. Then suddenly she refocused her gaze on me.

"Ooooohh," she sighed, as tears spilled out onto her cheek. "Sometimes the grief strikes hard. I had some beautiful canoe rides with Mike."

"It's okay, Karen," I said, moving toward her, giving her an affectionate hug.

"When can you come?" she asked, smiling again.

In all her growing up, Karen has not lost the spontaneity of childhood. She might be happy one moment, sad the next. Her down times don't seem to last long, not nearly as long as mine do. Karen can giggle and cry several times in one day without skipping a beat to her truthful, almost-always-optimistic heart song. No need to deny her feelings like fear and sadness. Of course, she's shed some tears now and then, as any human being would. But Karen seems to have the ability to center her thoughts, again and again, on positive truths.

The ability to look at life optimistically has something to do with temperament and body chemistry too, so if you're not a generally positive person, don't be discouraged. Maybe you're more like me, and you have to make a conscious effort to guard yourself from getting stuck in negative thinking, to pray often to see things from God's truthful perspective. This is the important thing: Be genuine, striving to focus on the positive, yet never just act upbeat and optimistic at the expense of truthfulness. Remember my Adventures in La-la Land? During those days, I was a "Pollyanna" in the sense I'd often accused The Glad Girl of being. Somewhere along the way, I lost the noble quest for emotional integrity I'd had at the ripe age of twelve, and reverted to the game of make-believe.

Do you know someone who, as an adult, has Glad Game optimism, yet is not a phony? As women, when someone puts on a happy front that isn't really working for them, we can sniff it out intuitively. Again, that's what bothers us—phoniness, not optimism.

Although there may be a miniscule number of people who are so positive they're minimally affected by life's deepest tragedies, most of us won't fall into that category. But you know what? It really doesn't matter. We don't have to fake it and say that our circumstances are positive when they really are not. Sometimes, the only thing to be glad about is remembering that we have God's company and His love. And that alone is reason enough to "rejoice and be glad." In fact, it's the very best reason of all, because our gladness has nothing to do with our circumstances. It depends solely on our keeping our eyes on Jesus, and setting our minds on His truth.

Charles Stanley tells a story of a time when he was so discouraged in his ministry, he was actually considering quitting. Week after week, an older woman in his congregation persistently asked Dr. Stanley to join her for Sunday lunch. Weary of her invitations, he agreed to go, mostly just to shut her up. Before they sat down to dinner, the woman led Dr. Stanley over to a picture in her hallway. It was a painting of Daniel in the lions' den, with a representation of God standing beside him.

"Look at this picture and tell me what you see," the woman said.

"Well, I see Daniel, and I see lions, and there are some torches burning in the background."

"You're missing the point, son," the woman said. "What I want you to see is that Daniel doesn't have his eyes on the lions." She pointed to the painting. "He's looking straight at God."

Dr. Stanley said he went home, got down on his knees, and asked for help in centering his mind-set on God. He credits this event as a life-changing encounter that shifted his focus from life's circumstances to the truth of God's reality.

wisdom of old

King Nebuchadnezzar placed Daniel in a high position in Babylon and lavished many gifts on him. Daniel asked the king to appoint Shadrach, Meshach, and Abednego as administrators, which he did. Sometime later, the king made a ninety-foot image of gold and commanded all the people in the nation to fall down and worship the image. Whoever did not fall down and worship the image was to be thrown into a fiery furnace.

But Shadrach, Meshach, and Abednego refused to bow down and worship the golden image, saying: "If we are thrown into the blazing furnace, the God we serve is able to save us from it, and he will rescue us from your hand, O king. But even if he does not, we want you to know, O king, that we will not serve your gods or worship the image of gold you have set up" (Daniel 3:17-18).

> *The greatest honor we can give Almighty God is to live gladly because of the knowledge of His love.*[5]
>
> *Julian of Norwich*

This passage has always warmed my heart (no pun intended). As Shadrach, Meshach, and Abednego affirmed their commitment to God, they were drop-dead sure of His character. *Even if He did not rescue them,* they would still not betray Him. God certainly *could* save them, but they also knew He might not. As you probably know, God did intervene. Shadrach, Meshach, and Abednego lived through the blazing fire and came out unharmed, without a single trace of burns or scorches. They didn't even smell like smoke.

When our lives aren't going well, we may not be able to find anything the least bit optimistic in our circumstances. It is at these times when we most need to renew that glimpse of the Savior in our hearts as

Daniel did, to see God in the center of our lives. He is with us. He loves us. He tenderly cares for us. These are bottom line reasons to "rejoice and be glad." This is genuine Glad Girl optimism—positive truth that will endure throughout eternity.

> *Though the fig tree does not bud*
> *and there are no grapes on the vines,*
> *though the olive crop fails*
> *and the fields produce no food,*
> *though there are no sheep in the pen*
> *and no cattle in the stalls,*
> *yet I will rejoice in the Lord,*
> *I will be joyful in God my Savior.*
> *The Sovereign Lord is my strength;*
> *he makes my feet like the feet of a deer,*
> *he enables me to go on the heights.*

Habakkuk 3:17-19

timeless stories

of

FRIENDS as MENTORS

chapter six

SACRIFICIAL LOVE

"Your success . . . was my success."

Charlotte

Charlotte's Web
by E.B. White

In the well-loved children's classic *Charlotte's Web,* a pig named Wilbur meets Charlotte, a spidery kind of mentor. As they become neighbors in Mr. Arable's barn cellar, Charlotte offers Wilbur hope, encouragement, and eventually, sacrificial love.

Wilbur's first impression of Charlotte was that she was a bloodthirsty predator. This proved inaccurate, as so many first impressions do, and it didn't take long for Wilbur to warm up to Charlotte's caring ways.

"It's a miracle," people exclaimed when they saw words spelled out in a spider's web. SOME PIG had been intricately woven into Charlotte's web, which hung directly over Wilbur's resting spot. It seemed a supernatural declaration of Wilbur's greatness.

However, as time passed, Mr. Arable forgot that Wilbur was "some pig." When he grew to a not-so-little size, it appeared Wilbur was destined for the sausage house. But more woven wonder-words appeared in Charlotte's web: TERRIFIC, HUMBLE, and RADIANT. Always woven directly above Wilbur's bed of hay, always invoking an abundance of pig-praise from neighbors and passers-by.

He who walks with the wise grows wise.
Proverbs 13:20a

Charlotte's concern for Wilbur, a runt pig in need of her aid, quickly grew into love. Spinning messages to insure Wilbur's survival and well-being became Charlotte's mission in life. Eventually, as is usually the case when one finds a good mentor, Charlotte's own character strengths were reproduced in Wilbur.

Nobody ever discovered it was the spider who was responsible for the barnyard miracle.

"Charlotte . . . why are you so quiet?" asked Wilbur, as Charlotte grew weaker and weaker from all her days of spinning.

"I like to sit still," replied Charlotte, trying to conceal her failing strength. "I've always been rather quiet."

"Yes, but you seem specially so today. Do you feel all right?"

"A little tired, perhaps. But I feel peaceful," said Charlotte. "Your success in the ring this morning was, to a small degree, my success. Your future is assured."[1]

mentor's wisdom

Charlotte worked hard into the wee hours of the morning spinning strands of encouragement for Wilbur because she loved him. More than any words could ever say, Charlotte communicated sacrificial love through the way she lived. Her actions—giving time and energy beyond what she really had for another's well-being—her deeds of kindness on Wilbur's behalf far exceeded the power of spoken or written words when it came to showing love. Charlotte was a mentor who gave herself. When I think of people who love sacrificially, by giving of themselves, a woman named Linda comes to mind.

IN LOVE'S SERVICE

Linda was a therapist-in-training. Unable to have children of her own, she turned her time and energy toward nurturing other women in need of emotional healing. An incurable viral condition had severely weakened Linda's body and mercilessly attacked her immune system, requiring her to stay at home most of the time and keep to a strict diet of whole foods and pure fruit juices.

A friend of mine named Marcie was privileged to be one of Linda's first clients. The two of them met weekly in Linda's home for the better part of a year to work through issues of Marcie's disillusionment in her marriage. As Marcie eagerly gave me weekly summations of her counseling sessions, I noted it was not so much Linda's wise words of insight that impressed Marcie. Instead, she was deeply impressed by her counselor's tenderheartedness and sincere desire to help.

"Sometimes Linda was not able to get out of bed and dress, so we talked by phone," Marcie said to me one day. "At the beginning of each of our visits, she would always pray for the ability to be, symbolically, the compassionate arms of Christ extended to me."

When Linda's husband, a pastor, was transferred to a church in another city, Marcie lost contact with her mentor. "I recall her graying hair and emaciated frame," Marcie mused. "She seemed to be aging rapidly, far beyond her years. Yet she gave whatever energy she had to a few fortunate people like me, who didn't deserve such compassionate care, but who were in need of sacrificial love." Marcie went on to say that she sensed something powerful when she was in Linda's presence. It was as if

Linda had something intangible and transcendent to give her, something she had gotten from God. Marcie believed the comfort she received in Linda's presence was actually the comfort of Christ—His arms extended to Marcie through Linda's presence.

Such is the nature of sacrificial love—giving something beyond your own resources to people who don't necessarily deserve it, but who need compassionate care. Like Wilbur, Marcie realized she was the recipient of a gift she could never earn or repay. For Linda, loving others was just a way of life.

> *Why did you do all this for me?" asked Wilbur. "I don't deserve it. I've never done anything for you."*
>
> *"You have been my best friend," replied Charlotte. "That in itself is a tremendous thing."*

—————⌘—————

> *Praise be to the God and Father of our Lord Jesus Christ, the Father of compassion and the God of all comfort, who comforts us in all our troubles, so that we can comfort those in any trouble with the comfort we ourselves have received from God.*
>
> 2 Corinthians 3:4

Have you ever felt you were giving to another from the depth of your personal resources, even beyond yourself, loving sacrificially? Maybe you gave time and comfort to a friend in need of compassion. Or perhaps you did some laborious physical work, even when you were exhausted, for another's well-being. Demonstrations of sacrificial love call to my mind a play, *The Angel That Troubled the Waters,* after the story of Jesus healing a man at the Pool of Bethesda.

The time is the early 1900s; the place is the courtyard around the Pool of Bethesda. Every so often an angel comes to stir the water, and the sick and lame people surrounding the pool try to be first to get in the water so they can be healed. One of the people, the only one who has been there since the beginning, is a severely depressed physician.

Each day the elderly doctor tries to be first to enter the pool after the angel has moved the waters. But by the time the old, weakened man gets out of his chair, straightens his back, and hobbles down to the pool, someone has always beat him.

Then one day, just after the angel has rippled the waters, the physician is especially light on his feet. It seems as if his lifelong dream is about to come true. He rushes to the pool and is first to reach the water's edge. But just as his toes are about to touch the water, a voice calls out, "Stop!" The old man pulls his foot back to the side of the pool. "Stop! Move back!" It is the angel. "This healing is not for you," the angel continues, moving closer to the elderly physician as he collapses helplessly into a chair. "It is your very pain that makes you the healing physician that you are."

Each day for many years, the old man had hoped to be healed. Now, as he slumps in his chair, a knowing expression slowly begins to spread across his face, perhaps a new resolve, a deeper understanding than he has ever known. His very pain is the sacrifice he must pay for the ability to heal others.

At this point, perhaps the physician felt a little like Charlotte after all her hours of spinning—tired, but peaceful. He had that same deep desire to help others, but he had probably never thought of its coming through his pain.

Then the angel concludes with an unexpected message, reminding the audience that healing and sacrificial giving are not always what they appear to be: "In love's service, only the wounded can serve." *Only the wounded?* the people silently wonder, perhaps having clung to lifelong inner assumptions that it's only the strong who serve. As in the military, where the wounded are given an honorable discharge—recognized, yet dismissed. But in God's service, the wounded (which includes all of us sooner or later, to greater and lesser degrees) can serve effectively, meaningfully, sacrificially, as Charlotte served Wilbur.

In fact, anyone who brings real comfort to others must give up (though not always voluntarily), his or her illusion of complete wholeness, total healing in this life. Because it is the wounded who have a need to go and get the comfort from the God of all compassion, and then to pass it on to others. Henri Nouwen, author *of The Wounded Healer*, put it this way:

> *The minister is called to recognize the sufferings of his time in his own heart and make that recognition the starting point of his service. Whether he tries to enter into a dislocated world, relate to a convulsive generation, or speak to a dying man, his service will not be perceived as authentic unless it comes from a heart wounded by the suffering about which he speaks. Thus nothing can be written about ministry without a deeper understanding of the ways in which the minister can make his own wounds available as a source of healing.*[2]

What are the wounds you have suffered? Have you ever realized that God can use your very pain—your particular version of woundedness, whether it is a battle with an eating disorder, the loss of a child, a divorce—to bring comfort to others around you? To offer yourself for the comfort of others in this way is a huge sacrifice on your part, but if it's done according to God's leading, He will use your life, not just *in spite of* your pain and suffering, but *through* it.

⸺ ◦◦◦ ⸺

Maybe your way of giving uncensored affection is not quite as dramatic as the physician's story, yet equally noteworthy as one of the ways God calls His children to love others sacrificially. Perhaps you are a person like Dick, a kindhearted man who unselfishly cared for his wife, Nell, for over twenty years. Nell was a dear friend who died a couple of years ago after suffering twenty-plus years with rheumatoid arthritis. All I have left of her are my memories, but I will treasure them always. Of all the experiences we enjoyed together, one of my favorites was watching children's movies. We'd sit for hours in front of Nell's TV and mindlessly poke popcorn into our mouths, never taking our eyes off the screen.

One evening we planned to get together with our husbands for an informal meal and a movie at Nell and Dick's house. "Hi, Bren! Hey, Frank, come on in." Dick waved from the wooden front porch of their doublewide mobile home.

"Oh good, you're here," Nell greeted us as we entered the patio door. "I wonder if there are any kids who enjoy watching these old children's movies as much as we old fogies do," Nell chuckled from her wheelchair, impatient for our pizza and video night to begin.

As I plopped the pizza box down onto the kitchen counter, I caught a whiff of the popcorn Dick was preparing to go with the movie.

"You get the pizza out, Bren," Dick said, "and I'll serve up the popcorn and Cokes." As I reached for the stack of paper plates, I noticed that Dick had an extra-wide black belt around his waist.

"What's that?" I asked curiously, as I pulled apart two cheesy slices of pizza.

"Back brace," Dick replied. "Gotta wear it until the pain stops." Dick wasn't one for long, detailed explanations when it came to his own pain or discomfort. His life revolved around caring for Nell, and nothing else mattered as much as *her* comfort.

"Are you okay?" I asked, concerned.

"Oh, yeah, I'm just gonna have to wear this thing and do some exercises to strengthen my back muscles so I can keep on lifting Nell."

"Sounds like you need more than a back brace to me," Frank chimed in. "You need some help, Dick?"

"Naaah," Dick said, smiling. "Just your prayers. That'll do." With that, the subject was closed and we settled comfortably into overstuffed chairs with our pizza, popcorn, and Cokes. It was show time, and *Anne of Green Gables* was our film of choice for the evening. Before long, though, the sound of gentle snoring punctuated the background. It was Dick. He'd fallen asleep in his recliner just after he'd eaten, kicked back, and put his feet up.

As the movie continued, Dick's soft snoring served as a gentle, comforting reminder of his presence. Nell and I chatted throughout the first half of the video, then decided that with Dick asleep and Frank on the way, we'd wait until another time to watch the rest. As I clicked off the television, Dick awoke with a start. "Oh! Is it over?" he asked, scratching the side of his head.

"Nope," Nell replied, "but they've got to go home." After I collected the pizza plates and Frank set the Coke glasses in the sink, we walked through the sliding glass patio door to their wooden porch, hugged, and said our good-nights. The golden glow of the porch light shone cheerily on a clay pot full of cherry tomatoes, adding a colorful, final touch to our farewell greeting.

"Take care, and come back soon!" Dick shouted after us as we backed out of the driveway.

As I think back over days with Dick and Nell, I realize that although Nell had lots of friends, people hardly noticed all the hard work Dick did behind the scenes to keep her as comfortable as possible. He never seemed to need a thank-you. Dick's daily routine began in midmorning (he and Nell were night owls, so they slept in until about ten), when he fixed Nell's breakfast and helped her bathe.

Dick did his best to lift his ailing wife in and out of the tub, massage her shoulders with a small vibrator, help her dress, and get her into her electric scooter. Then it was time for medications and breakfast, followed by cooking for the day. Dick had his hands full—that's for sure!

When friends offered to bring a meal or help with chores around the house, he graciously accepted, but otherwise he just went about his business without complaint. "Her joy is my joy," I once heard Dick say. That truth rang truer each passing month as I observed Dick tirelessly care for

Nell and encourage her with his cheerful, often humorous words. He had a sort of "whistle-while-you-work" attitude. Dick's very life demonstrated, day-to-day, how to love somebody sacrificially.

When Nell died at age seventy-four, Dick hardly knew what to do with himself.

"I was the one who gained the most from living with her," he said through tears following Nell's funeral. "She was such a jewel of a person to be with." In time, Dick went to stay with family in another state, and we talked only occasionally by phone, or exchanged cards and letters.

After a few months, we heard the sad news that he needed more consistent care and had to be placed in a nursing home. I am quite sure, however, that Dick's giving spirit is at work even in that setting. As long as Dick has presence of mind, he'll be blessing and caring for others around him. That's just the way it works with people who understand sacrificial love.

Fond memories of Nell and Dick resurface now and then, as I recall Dick's words so fondly spoken, "Her joy was my joy." They linger in my mind, and swirl together with similar sentiments from our storybook mentor, Charlotte: "Your success . . . was my success."

I have often wondered how I would respond if I had an invalid husband or an aging mother who depended on me for care. What would my attitude be?

> *I Wonder*
> *You know, Lord, how I serve You*
> *With great emotional fervor*
> *In the limelight.*
> *You know how eagerly I speak for You*
> *At a women's club.*
> *You know how I effervesce when I promote*
> *A fellowship group.*
> *You know my genuine enthusiasm*

At a Bible study.
But how would I react, I wonder
If You pointed to a basin of water
And asked me to wash the callused feet
Of a bent and wrinkled old woman
Day after day
Month after month
In a room where nobody saw
And nobody knew.[3]

Ruth Harms Calkin

w i s d o m   o f   o l d

His victory is my victory.[4]

Corrie ten Boom

In the Garden of Gethsemane, Jesus prepared Himself to become the supreme sacrifice of all time. From God's heart flowed a love that would give up His own Son for the redemption of our sins. "My soul is overwhelmed with sorrow to the point of death," Jesus said to His disciples. And then He prayed, "My Father, if it is not possible for this cup to be taken away unless I drink it, may your will be done" (Matthew 26:38, 42).

Sacrificial love.

The compassionate heart of God seems to be tilted toward the underdog—the runt of the litter like Wilbur, the weakling in need of defense. Jesus Christ was sacrificially given so that the miracle of God's love could be multiplied to cover sins of people like me and like you. It's easy for us as Christians to take this outrageous sacrifice for granted, to glibly recite words from passages such as John 3:16 without letting the precious cost of God's gift sink into our minds and hearts. He paid a radical price for our sins. Perhaps even ridiculous.

On a recent Sunday morning, my pastor told a story of Frederick Buechner's disgust when one day he saw the words "Jesus saves" written on a dirty concrete wall among vulgar expressions and crude graffiti. It was as if the name of Christ had been slung into the gutter. Upon reflection, Buechner realized this is exactly what God did when He sent Jesus to pay for our sins. He, who was blameless, was cast into the muck and shame of our worst sins.

Charlotte . . . why are you so quiet?" asked Wilbur. "Do you feel all right?"

"A little tired, perhaps," replied Charlotte. "But . . . your future is assured."

In the same way, God's extravagant sacrifice assures the future of His children.

Loving people like Linda and Dick can show others dim reflections of God's sacrificial love as demonstrated both in the life and in the death of Jesus Christ.

It all began with His birth two thousand years ago in another kind of animal shelter. Not a barn cellar, but a lowly stable. God's only Son was born to become sacrificial love personified. In this true story, it was a star that shone above the child on a bed of hay, instead of a spider's web above a pig's resting-place. A bright, shining star pointing down to the infant Jesus.

This is how much God loved the world: He gave his Son, his one and only Son. And this is why: so that no one need be destroyed. By believing in him, anyone can have a whole and lasting life.

John 3:16 (TM)

Radiant.

Humble.

Some Savior.

chapter seven

CONFIDENCE

"I think I can, I think I can,

I think I can, I think I can."

The Little Blue Engine

The Little Engine That Could
by   Watty   Piper

Chug, chug, chug. Puff, puff, puff. Ding-dong, ding-dong. A train loaded with oodles of toys and good food for the good boys and girls on the other side of the mountain merrily puffed along. All of a sudden, the train stopped with a jerk, unable to go any farther. Try as it might, the little train could not get its wheels to turn.

So the funny little clown enlisted the support of all the dolls and toys aboard to cry out together for help. "Please, won't you please pull our train over the mountain?" they asked the Shiny New Engine. The Little Train explained its worthy mission, but to no avail. The Shiny New Engine thought he was too important to help the likes of the little train. So the dolls and toys asked others for help—The Big Strong Engine and the Rusty Old Engine. "I cannot. I cannot," they replied.

Just then, along came the Little Blue Engine. She was quite small, but she chug, chug, chugged along, stopping with a jerk when she saw the little train.

"What is the matter?" she asked kindly.

"Oh, Little Blue Engine! Will you pull us over the mountain?" the dolls and toys asked. "Please, please, help us, Little Blue Engine."

"I'm not very big," replied the Little Blue Engine. "They use me only for switching trains in the yard. I have never been over the mountain."

"But we must get over the mountain before the children awake," said the dolls and toys. "The good boys and girls on the other side won't have any toys to play with or good food to eat unless you help us. Please, please help us, Little Blue Engine."

Now, the Little Blue Engine was not very big. She had never been used for anything very important. But as she thought about the children on the other side of the mountain, and how they would not have toys and food without someone's help, she decided to hitch herself onto the little train and make her best effort to pull it up and over.

So the Little Blue Engine tugged and pulled, pulled and tugged, slowly starting off. Puff, puff, chug, chug, she began to roll along. "I think I can, I think I can, I think I can, I think I can," she said. Up, up, up she climbed until at last she reached the top of the mountain. "Hurray! Hurray!" cried the dolls and toys. The Little Blue Engine had done it!

As she puffed back down the mountain, the Little Blue Engine smiled and seemed to say to herself, "I thought I could, I thought I could, I thought I could, I thought I could."[1]

mentor's wisdom

I recall reading this children's classic to my sons when they were preschoolers, over twenty-five years ago. Although I've always liked the story, I didn't seriously consider it for inclusion in this book at first glance, because it struck me as overly simplistic, not really worthy of pondering. But as I let my thoughts take me beneath the surface of the book's message, I discovered profound nuggets of biblical truth in the story of *The Little Engine That Could*.

For example, even though the Little Blue Engine felt inadequate for the task of pulling the train over the mountain, she was somehow able to muster a call for inner confidence by saying to herself, "I think I can." If the Engine shared our human frailties like insecurity, don't you know there had to be a Ping-Pong dialog going on in her head? It probably went something like this: *I think I can. But it's impossible. Oh, can I really? Yes, I think I can.*

Do you ever struggle in this way, batting opposing thoughts of confidence and insecurity back and forth in your mind? During our younger years, most of us picked up some negative programming that just sort of turns itself on automatically when we aren't feeling very strong or important. For me, it's the critical voice of my mom saying things like, "You'll never amount to anything," or "Can't you ever do anything right?" Although I now know she only meant to issue a warning, there are still days when I catch myself automatically tracking on this self-defeating detour before I even have time to think about it.

Our storybook mentor didn't feel very capable or powerful either, but she chose to give the task her all. Pulling the trainload of toys and food to the children on the other side of the mountain was an extremely worthwhile cause, deserving the little engine's best effort. Nothing less would do. Even when she was not sure she could succeed, the Little Blue Engine gained confidence by thinking of the worthy cause she was serving, and telling herself "I think I can" with every forward thrust of her unsure wheels.

91

I THINK I CAN

You probably know a person who exudes inner strength, modeling quiet confidence. Confident women and men, models of inspiration, are some-

times found in the most unlikely places. Just the other day as I was leaf-
ing through the *Dallas Morning News*, I came across a story about a man
who reminded me of *The Little Engine That Could.*

At ninety-eight years of age, George Dawson could not read or
write. But now, four years later, he was about to give a reading of his first
book, *Life Is So Good,* at the prestigious Myerson Auditorium in Dallas.
The news article showcasing the event was accompanied by a picture of a
tall, slightly stooped elderly man wearing a porkpie hat.

According to the article, a social service worker had canvassed
George's neighborhood a few years earlier in preparation for an offering of
adult literacy classes at the local high school. Throughout his lifetime,
George had convinced his kids he could ably assist them with their home-
work, although they knew he could only make a large X to sign his name.
Evidently George had subtly trained his children to ask their questions
orally, and he had no problem in the realm of spoken words. But reading
them was a different story. "I've lost a whole lot not knowing how to read,"
George said. "And not knowing how to count my money." Over the years,
he suspected a few people had taken advantage of him and paid him less
than he deserved, simply because he didn't know how to check the figures.

When the social worker offered George a chance to change all that,
he thought, *If I can read, I can find out for myself.* George had a growing
desire to be sure he and his family wouldn't be taken advantage of again
just because he couldn't read or write. Then again, could he really learn
to read at his age? With a bit of reluctance and a strong sense of deter-
mination, George made his decision. "I will be attending school."

The oldest student in the history of the Dallas Independent School
District, Mr. Dawson quickly became a celebrity among his classmates,
motivating young and old alike. "He gives me a lot of energy," said a
young classmate. "If *he* comes here to class, *I know* I can make it."

George Dawson's book was co-authored by Richard Glaubman of
Seattle, who told reporters that young people were intensely curious

about George's life. "The kids wanted to know, 'Is he a second-grader? What size desk does he sit in? How did a man that age gain the confidence to learn to read? What was his life like?' "

Despite becoming a published author, George Dawson continued to attend adult literacy classes, encouraging others to learn all they could while there was still time. The motto spelled out in large letters across one of the classroom walls in the room where George was interviewed by the news reporter may well have described the main theme of his life: *You never fail until you quit trying.* At 102, this man was still trying new things. Even though, to this point, he'd never been particularly important in the eyes of the public, he was attempting things most people forty years his junior would not have even thought about trying. He was still saying, "I think I can. I think I can."[2]

As a woman, do you have that kind of confidence? Can you respond to inner longings to attain something you've wanted to learn, perhaps a new skill you've wanted to acquire for as long as you can remember? If you have that "I think I can" spirit, as George Dawson did, you've overcome some of your fear of risking failure.

But all of us still have some things to learn about acquiring real, enduring inner confidence. Let's look to our storybook mentor, *The Little Engine That Could.* I believe she can lead us to insights about our spiritual lives, whether we're merrily chugging along on a steady, gradual climb, or approaching the most formidable of mountains.

"I think I can, I think I can, I think I can, I think I can!" said the Little Engine. Somewhere along the path to maturity, the confidence we once had as children begins to waver. Although each woman's "train of thought" travels a slightly different track, her inner self-talk sometimes descends from "I think I can" to something more along the lines of "I probably can't but I'm afraid to find out for sure, so I won't even try," or

"Uh-oh, I didn't, I knew I couldn't." Those who have given up trying may need a gentle reminder that "God's grace covers failure, but cannot make up for passivity. We have to do our part. The sin God rebukes is not trying and failing, but failing to try."[3]

At twenty-eight, Holly was convinced she would never find a good job. An average student, she'd worked hard to graduate from college, earn a teaching certificate, and get an apartment of her own. Then she had a couple of bad experiences in her first teaching positions. "I've already failed in two different school districts," she said one day as we talked over lunch. "I'm afraid to try another full-time position."

Holly moved back in with her parents, deciding to play it safe and accept only substitute teaching assignments—not necessarily a bad idea.

But now, four years after her graduation, her fear of another job failure kept her from trying again. When it came to her vocational search, Holly was letting passivity sit behind the wheel of her engine car, rather than trying to get herself back on track.

> *Apart from me you can do nothing.*
> Jesus in John 15:5b

Holly's story has a happy ending, however. When her brother, eight years younger than she, was suddenly stricken with an operable brain tumor, Holly's attitude changed abruptly. The prognosis for his recovery was good, but included immediate surgery and radiation treatments following. The family's medical bills increased dramatically. Only part of her brother's treatment would be covered under their family insurance, and Holly wanted to help.

It wasn't long before she was out looking for a job, and of course, she found one quickly. The job turned out to be a great new beginning, not a perfect position, but one that got her started again in the right direction. For Holly, as with the Little Blue Engine, a worthy cause was just what it took to get her off the passivity track, chugging along again, saying, "I think I can."

For other women, who have achieved a good deal of success

throughout life and base their self-assurance on their personal triumphs, it can be easy to get sidetracked about what real confidence is. Long lists of "shoulds," "musts," and "oughts" may begin to fuel the perfectionist's engine. Her self-talk sounds more like "I must, because I sure can't depend on anyone else," or "I'd better, because I'm worthless if I don't." But sooner or later, we grow weary from huffing and puffing and chugging along on our own steam. Eventually, all of these tracks lead into the Roundhouse of Inadequacy where we finally derail, having met up with feelings of inferiority, insecurity, and self-defeat.

Whether you've derailed on the track of passivity, or you're off blazing your own track, thinking you're quite adequate running on your own steam, I'd like to tell you about a little saying I once heard from a friend. It goes like this: "I can't. He never said I could. He can. He always said He would."

These words of truth have stuck with me through the years and give me a solid reminder that God knows I am inadequate for whatever work He sends my way. He's known all along. I'm the one who may have trouble remember-

> *If we cannot do it without God, it means we do it with God if we do it at all.*[4]
>
> *Lewis Smedes*

ing. I'm the one who is tempted again and again to say "I think I can" without linking up with Him as the Engine empowering my journey.

THE GAME OF LIFE

Were you ever on a baseball team? I opted for the cheerleading route myself, preoccupied throughout my girlhood days with popularity and looks, unable to see the benefits of working up a sweat just to bat and chase a ball. I overlooked the value of competition, unless it was for homecoming queen or "most popular." But now I see that I missed some really important lessons by not learning more about baseball as a young girl.

For one, failure is a natural, normal part of the game. Errors are even counted and posted on a public scoreboard! This all-American game can also teach us that when we make a mistake, it doesn't mean we're no good, or that we're not on the team anymore. Mistakes don't even keep players from winning the game. Good lessons, huh?

"You can do it!" shout the fans in the grandstands. Even at the end of a lost game, a good coach might say, "That's okay, we'll get 'em next time!" Did you learn this kind of wisdom during your girlhood days? If not, perhaps you are more like me, and as the years passed and you made mistakes, your errors piled up. You began to feel inadequate, judging yourself unworthy, incapable, not okay. To compensate, maybe you gave up, or maybe you tried even harder, pushing yourself relentlessly and allowing no space in your perfectly successful-looking life for a single failure.

For the Lord will be your confidence and will keep your foot from being snared.

Proverbs 3:26

If this is the way you played the game, mistakes came to mean worthlessness as a person. Errors were concealed as dark secrets on a scary night. Thoughts of others finding out about your mistakes began to haunt you. Even God Himself seemed terribly let down by you, disgusted with all your failures. The big-league bully of inadequacy had stolen the fun of your carefree innings of life.

But God (who I believe, incidentally, probably loves baseball) never expected us to be adequate. He always knew we were not strong, that we'd make lots of errors. He has known from the beginning of time that there would be days when it would take incredible inner strength for us to utter words of confidence and say, "I think I can." Days when everything would be going wrong, when the people we love would turn their backs on us, or when we'd strike out in the last inning of a love relationship.

Being merciful and loving, God made us in such a way that we need Him as our head coach to live our lives well, and we need a game plan beyond the scope of our own lives. If we are to have inner confidence, it has to come from Him. Further, we need to realize that making mistakes and feeling inadequate do not mean we are put out of the game; they are just a gentle call to help us remember our need of Him as our Source.

THE GIFT OF INADEQUACY

I once heard Joni Eareckson Tada talk about how hard it is sometimes just to have a smile for people in the audience when she speaks publicly. Her early morning routine begins with the arrival of a friend who bathes, dresses, and feeds Joni her breakfast. One particular morning, as Joni awoke, her shoulders were aching and sore, as they so often were.

"Lord, I am so tired of all this pain," she cried out. "I'd really rather You'd just take me home to be with You, instead of leaving me here where I can only tell people about You. I don't even have a smile for anyone today, I'm just hurting." Of course, there was no audible answer. Then she added, "But Lord, if You want me to go out there and give those people a smile, You're gonna need to give me one, because I don't have one today."

Have you ever felt empty, insignificant, completely out of fuel? At such a time, you may have been like Joni, saying, "God, I can't." Actually,

> *For you have been my . . . confidence since my youth.*
> *Psalm 71:5*

this is a good thing to say, a great point of beginning, because it means *you qualify* to receive God's enabling power. When we realize our own inadequacy and turn to God, admitting we aren't up to the job at hand, He answers with, "That's okay, I always knew you couldn't, but if it's important to Me, I'll empower you to do it."

Suddenly, "I can't" becomes "I can," meaning "God and I can, by chugging along together." This is real, lasting confidence. It comes when we know the inadequacy of our own strength and resources.

Okay, we may say. *So, once I understand what confidence truly is, I can have it all the time, right?* Oh, how I wish it were this easy. But for some of us, placing confidence in our own abilities comes quite easily and naturally, and we get sidetracked more often than we'd like. Long-established ruts run deep.

But as soon as we realize we're placing our confidence in our own abilities, not linking up to God as our power source, we can quickly return to the track of His purposes. Chugging along to the tune of "I'd better, because I'm worthless if I don't" switches over to "I can if He wants me to, because He can." Ah, what a relief it is to have Him fueling my engine instead of trying to do it by myself.

> *Salvation is the change from being confident about our own efforts to the state in which we despair of doing any-*  *thing for ourselves and leave it to God.*[5]
>
> *C.S. Lewis*

When I surrender my life to God each morning, I usually find renewed confidence sprinkled over each day's helping of His mercy. Sometimes I won't be able to accomplish things I'd like to. Sometimes I won't get things I ask for. But if I entrust my life, will, and capabilities to Christ's care, I will be able to do many things I could not otherwise do, because of His power.

My emptiness is filled with His strength.

"I can't" becomes "I think I can."

wisdom of old

All of us feel inadequate at times, even heroes of the faith like Moses. In the third and fourth chapters of Exodus, God called to Moses from within a burning bush. "Moses! Moses!" The Lord was concerned about His people suffering under the hands of slave drivers. "I am sending you to Pharaoh to bring my people the Israelites out of Egypt."

But Moses said, "Who am I, that I should go to Pharaoh and bring the Israelites out of Egypt?"

God said, "I will be with you."

But Moses grasped for answers. "What if they ask me Your name? What shall I tell them? What if they do not believe me or listen to me . . . ? I have never been eloquent . . . I am slow of speech and tongue. O Lord, please send someone else to do it" (Exodus 3:13, 4:1,10).

I can do everything God asks me to with the help of Christ who gives me the strength and power.

Philippians 4:13
(TLB)

Although Moses eventually obeyed God, his first stammerings smacked of fear and inadequacy. "I can't."

It took awhile before he got on track with God, placing his confidence in Him. Perhaps he was more like us than we think, insecure at times, and he had to remember that God was the One who would make him adequate, because it was His purpose being fulfilled.

When you feel inadequate, remember that you are not alone. Even heroes of old like Moses sometimes had difficulty saying, "I think I can." Although it's true, you may not be able to do all you'd like to do in this life, God will faithfully empower you to do all that He calls you to do. In fact, if you realize you are inadequate to achieve His purposes by relying on your own capabilities alone, then you are blessed.

Blessed are those who know they cannot endlessly chug along on their own power. Blessed are those who feel inadequate, yet fall on their knees and surrender their hearts to God day after day, relying on Him for the ability to say, "I think I can." Blessed are those who place their confidence in God's strength and purposes rather than their own, and who are willing to try their best because God is the One empowering them, pulling them up, up, and over to the other side of the mountain.

Chug, chug. Puff, puff.

The Little Engine That Could rolls along, one wheel-turn at a time.

"I think I can, I think I can, I think I can, I think I can."

99

chapter eight

HUMILITY

I put down my head and threw my

whole weight against the collar.

I pulled the load steadily up the hill.

Black Beauty

Black Beauty
by Anna Sewell

lack Beauty is a story about a horse who lived a little more than a hundred years ago, told from his point of view. He spent the first three years of his life romping in the pasture with other colts, hearing stories about his ancestry from his mother. These stories about his strong family background, along with motherly instruction, would be an encouragement to him throughout his life, in good times and in bad.

"You have been well bred and well born," Beauty's mother told him frequently. "I hope you will grow up gentle and good, and never learn bad ways; do your work with a good will, lift your feet up well when you trot, and never bite or kick even in play."

After Beauty's first carefree years, he had to learn to live under the rule of his masters as he grew into a workhorse, standing in a stall until a man had need of him. In those days, horseback riding was not just a recreational pastime, as it is today. Horses were a part of the everyday life of people, who depended on them for transportation and business. Beauty was obedient and cooperative with his masters, just as his mother had told him to be. Besides that, he was smart. Sometimes, when judgment calls had to be made, such as whether or not to try to cross an engorged stream during a flood, Beauty was wiser than his masters. He even saved them from disaster on occasion, though the horse seldom got credit for his acts of valor.

Throughout Beauty's lifetime he was sold repeatedly, passed around from decent folk to cruel grooms and indifferent masters. It was John Manley, a gentle and kind man, who gave a name to the black stallion with the white blaze upon his forehead. Another owner was Jerry, a London cab driver, a wonderful man with a loving family. But then there was Reuben, who drank too much. *If people only knew what a comfort a light hand is,* the horse often thought, *they'd not poke and whip us so much.*

Getting on in years, Black Beauty was again up for sale. He hoped to find good work with good food and fair treatment from a master. He was sold to a corn dealer, who seemed nice enough. But the master was often away from home, and the driver grossly overloaded Beauty, sometimes abusing him. If he'd had to serve under that cruel driver very much longer, it surely would have been the end of him. Fortunately, a kind and understanding lady noticed Beauty and put a stop to the driver's cruelty. Beauty recounts his last day with the corn dealer's driver:

"Get on, you lazy fellow, or I'll make you," shouted the driver. *Then he laid the whip on badly. Again, I started the heavy load. I struggled on a few yards. Again the whip came down, and again I struggled forward. The pain of that great cart whip was sharp.*

"Oh, pray do not whip your good horse anymore!" said the compassionate lady, perhaps saving Beauty's life. "I am sure he is doing all he can, and the road is very steep. He cannot use all his power with his head held back as it is with that bearing rein. If you would take it off, I am sure he would do better."

The rein was taken off, and in a moment I put my head down to my very knees. What a comfort it was. Then I tossed it up and down several times to get the stiffness out of my neck. I put down my head and threw my whole weight against the collar. I spared no strength. I pulled the load steadily up the hill, and then stopped to take a breath.

"I am sure he is a fine-tempered creature," said the lady. "I daresay he has known better days. . . . We have no right to distress any of God's creatures." The woman stroked Beauty's neck. "We call them dumb animals, and so they are, for they cannot tell us how they feel, but they do not suffer less because they have no words."

Beauty was traded for a younger, stronger workhorse, only to find himself once more in the hands of a hard-driving, abusive owner. At last, the aging horse was bought by Farmer Thoroughgood, who fed him well and nursed him back to health.

Black Beauty spent his last days in a happy home with three kind ladies, doing reasonable and pleasant work. He was a horse who found internal rewards in being the best worker he could possibly be, following in the steps of his well-bred ancestors, humbly placing himself under the authority of a plethora of masters. While he was most grateful for the merciful owners, he always made his best work effort, whether life was carefree and just, or bitter and painful.[1]

m e n t o r ' s   w i s d o m

When *Black Beauty* first began his long stint of working years, he must have sorely missed the liberty he'd once enjoyed, running free in green pastures. How hard it must have been for this magnificent, high-spirited, well-bred animal to be reduced to the captivity of man's needs. Once confined to the stall except when working, Beauty had plenty of time to recall the earlier days when his mother told him stories about his ancestors. A sweet-tempered grandmother, a grandfather who won the cup two years at the Newmarket races. A gentle mother. A father with a great name—what a pedigree!

Black Beauty's life unfolded with blessed beginnings. It was this early memory of a good mother and a strong father that gave the horse the inner strength to humble himself, without ever losing his central sense of worth.

HUMILITY—WHAT IS IT?

What is humility? Is it believing that we are of no significance compared with everyone else? I don't think so. Is it inviting abuse? Again, I think not. Although it may seem contradictory, I believe true humility begins when we understand our own personal, spiritual pedigree. It begins with a quiet, internal confidence of our worth before our Father that nothing, no human being, can ever take from us. Being thoroughly convinced of our value in the eyes of our Father (though this may be more difficult for human beings than for animals), we find strength in ourselves that enables us to be more gracious to others. We can more readily shake off the heavy burden of needing applause of people, and plow on with doing whatever job we are called to do—whether that means speaking to thousands or scrubbing the floor. And when others mistreat us, humility is that miraculous quality that strengthens us within, helping us endure without losing our sense of value. Just as Black Beauty carried on in the reputation of his strong family line, we plod along steadily, knowing we are the sons and daughters of the Champion of the Universe.

When I see people performing acts of true humility, I feel a profound respect for them and wish to be more like them in spirit. The word "humility" comes from the Greek word *hummus*, meaning brought down to earth. Many of the humble people who've graced this planet have reached out to others at the expense of their own comfort, pride, or finances. They are "down-to-earth" souls who care more about making a difference than making a dollar. Images of Mother Theresa come to mind. Or perhaps there's a more personal illustration of humility in your own life. Maybe a teacher or a coach who willingly, even joyfully, chose to give up a well-paying career to help you or someone you know. It may have been your own father or mother.

Rick Bragg, winner of the Pulitzer Prize in 1996, wrote a tribute of a book to his mother, a woman who humbly sacrificed her life for her family in small ways, every day, for decades. Rick admits that he is not the only child with this story to tell but that, "Anyone could tell it, anyone who had a momma who went eighteen years without a new dress so that her sons could have school clothes, who picked cotton in other people's fields and ironed other people's clothes and cleaned the mess in other people's houses, so that her children wouldn't have to live on welfare alone, so that one of them could climb up her backbone and escape the poverty and hopelessness that ringed them, free and clean."[2]

Humility seeks another's good, and sometimes that involves a choice to sacrifice our own comfort to do so. Notice the word *choice*—it is not a resignation. Mr. Bragg's mother could have given her children up for adoption. She could have run away or done the minimum required of her as a parent. But she dreamed of seeing her children free, and willingly allowed them to use "her backbone" to climb out of poverty, "free and clean."

Interestingly, God has a way, though it may take awhile, of exalting the truly humble. In fact the Apostle Peter wrote about this fascinating turn of spiritual events. "Humble yourselves, therefore, under God's mighty hand, that He may lift you up in due time" (1 Peter 5:6).

In the case of Rick Bragg's mother, the reward for her sacrifice would come, in part, through her son's own achievement and his resulting gratitude as a grown man. "I tell [this story]," wrote Bragg, "because there should be a record of my momma's sacrifice even if it means unleashing ghosts, because it is one of the few ways I can think of, beyond financing her new false teeth and making sure the rest of her life is without the deprivations of her past, to repay her for all the suffering and indignity she absorbed for us, for me."[3]

Perhaps you have temporarily put your own desires and dreams on hold as a sacrifice to help someone you love. Laura, a young doctor I recently met, worked hard to finish med school and begin a family practice. A year after she'd set up her office, she made a decision to put her career plans on hold indefinitely to homeschool her child, who was having adjustment problems. Her colleagues may have thought she was crazy, but she radiated inner peace because of the choice she made.

Maybe you're a young mom growing weary of changing dirty diapers, as Black Beauty grew weary of his daily, routine tasks. Though the job itself may be unpleasant, your motivation for doing it to serve your child's needs is nothing but pure beauty to your Heavenly Father. Any single moms out there, rising at the crack of dawn like a faithful workhorse? Sure, you'd rather be at home taking care of your own child instead of carting him or her off to the baby-

> *I put down my head and threw my whole weight against the collar. I pulled the load steadily up the hill, and then stopped to take a breath.*
>
> *Black Beauty*

sitter. But your kids need food, clothing, and shelter, and your love for them propels you through early morning traffic, one mile at a time.

THE BLESSING OF TRUE HUMILITY

I desire to be a humble person, don't you? But experiences that are most likely to produce humility in my spirit are not always things I would knowingly and willfully choose. However, there are a few people in this world, a holy handful of truly humble saints who, by choice, commit their lives to the service of others in Jesus' name. Do you know of one? I'll tell you about one of my favorites, one I've quoted several times in this book—a beloved Dutch priest, Henri Nouwen.

As a young man, Henri pursued an academic career, gaining public acclaim in positions at prestigious places like Notre Dame, Harvard, and Yale. But in his later years, Henri felt he was losing touch with the deepest truths of who he really was, becoming enslaved to the approval of his coworkers and acquaintances.

On an audio account of Henri's spiritual journey, he

> *As a spiritual experience, humility contains its own unique paradox: Those possessed by it do not realize that they do participate in it! And those who think they possess it most often have no idea what it is.*[4]
>
> Ernest Kurtz &
> Katherine Ketcham

explains that he felt he was aimlessly wandering around, begging people to convince him he was okay. Questions loomed in his mind and heart: *"Do you like who I am?" "Do you like what I write?" "Do you think I'm okay?"* Through this internal agonizing, God eventually led Henri to make a radical decision to serve a community of handicapped adults at L'Arche Daybreak, in Canada. He spent the last years of his life serving those less capable, less knowledgeable than himself, poorer than he was in so many ways. And yet, in serving these people who had a lower station in life than he, in bending down to reach out a hand to others less fortunate, Henri learned some of life's most profound lessons.

He tells a story of one such lesson he learned from a severely handicapped woman called Janet. It occurred just before a chapel service. In the still, quiet sanctuary, all of a sudden, Janet got up out of her seat and walked right up to him. "Henri, can you give me a blessing?" she asked.

"Okay, Janet," he replied automatically, tracing with his thumb the sign of the cross on her forehead.

"Oh, no," Janet protested vehemently. "That doesn't work. I want a real blessing," she said, stepping closer to Henri and laying her head on his chest. "A blessing." At that moment, Henri knew instinctively that Janet wanted a blessing she could *feel*. A blessing that could penetrate her heart. So, he placed his arms around Janet's shoulders, encircling her with the sleeves of his long robe, until she almost vanished in the ample folds.

Then he said, "Janet, I want you to know that you are God's beloved daughter. You are precious in God's eyes. Your beautiful smile, your kindness to the people in your house, and all the good things you do show us what a beautiful human being you are. . . . I want you to remember who you are: a very special person, deeply loved by God and all the people who are here with you."

> *Jesus comes not for the super-spiritual but for the wobbly and the weak-kneed who know they don't have it all together, and who are not too proud to accept the hand-out of amazin' grace.*[5]
>
> Brennan Manning

"Yes," Janet said, smiling to show her satisfaction. "Yes, Henri, I believe it!" From this profoundly handicapped woman, Henri learned something valuable about human nature, something he would have never learned at such places as Harvard and Yale.[6] Something Black Beauty learned from his mother. The greatest blessing, the one felt most deeply in the heart, is that quiet, internal confidence of our worth in the eyes of our Heavenly Father.

In serving others less fortunate and less capable than himself, Henri Nouwen became an earthly reflection of Jesus Christ, passing on a family blessing in a way a handicapped woman could understand it. During his final years of ministry at L'Arche, Henri learned many secrets of true greatness. And it was this priest's lesson of humility—this trading in of the silk robes of intelligentsia for the uniform of simplicity—that opened the door to beauty he'd never known in the halls of academia.

wisdom of old

In some ways, the scene of Black Beauty being beaten and abused reminds me of the way men cursed and whipped Jesus on His way to the cross. Here we have divinity in the form of a man with the most amazing pedigree that ever was, whose Father set the stars in the heavenlies. Yet He chose to humble Himself, enduring ultimate mistreatment. Not because He was forced to do so, but because He had a greater goal in mind, one He considered worth the sacrifice.

Jesus Christ came down low to planet Earth, allowed Himself to be molded into the clay form of a man, so He could see us eye to eye. He made a conscious choice to lower Himself to endure the pain and indignities of the cross. Although Jesus knew He was equal to God, He humbled Himself to a death on the cross. Note that Christ's humiliation involved an internal choice. He didn't have to endure this torture. He chose to do it out of love, to serve as a living sacrifice for you and for me. No one took His life from Him. He laid it down willingly.

They took Jesus away. Carrying his cross, Jesus went out to the place called Skull Hill, where they crucified him.

John 19:17 (TM)

This is the story of truest humility, of the One who willingly put His head down to pull the load of the cross on His bruised and beaten back, up a hill we know as Calvary.

"I put my head down . . . I pulled the weight steadily up the hill."

The words echo hauntingly, and linger in the stalls of my mind.

He has showed you, O man, what is good. And what does the Lord require of you? To act justly and to love mercy and to walk humbly with your God.

Micah 6:8

109

chapter nine

COMING ALIVE

"Don't let us talk about dying.

Let us talk about living."

Mary Lennox

The Secret Garden

by Frances Hodgson Burnett

After the sudden death of her parents, Mary Lennox was sent from her home in India to stay with her uncle, Mr. Archibald Craven, at Misselthwaite Manor, England. Mr. Craven was known as a kind but reclusive hunchback who went into hiding shortly after his wife's death following the birth of their son, Colin. Sad and lonely, Mary's only interest lay in a secret garden abandoned after Mrs. Craven's fatal accident there.

Soon after Mary arrived at Misselthwaite Manor, Mr. Craven introduced himself. "I am your guardian. Play out of doors as much as you like. It's a big place and you may go where you like and amuse yourself as you like." After a brief pause, he asked, "Is there anything you want?

Do you want toys, books, dolls?"

"Might I . . . might I have a bit of earth?" asked Mary.

"Earth!" What do you mean?"

"To plant seeds in—to make things grow—to see them come alive."

"You can have as much earth as you want," Mr. Craven said. "When you see a bit of earth you want, take it, child, and make it come alive."

In the secret garden, things that were once dormant or dead begin to come alive. First a friendly robin flits from post to post, guiding Mary to the hidden key to the garden door. Delighted by her discovery, Mary then gathers and plants seeds and waits for them to sprout from the rich soil.

She and a local boy named Dickon entice Mary's invalid cousin, Colin, with the "secrets" of the garden, planting a longing for a healthy, normal life in the heart of this child hypochondriac. For her own reasons, Colin's nurse had convinced the boy he was terribly ill. "Don't let us talk about dying. Let us talk about living," Mary chides Colin when he complains.

> *The garden is a proper place of the soul where beauty, contemplation, and quiet take precedence over the busier concerns of daily life.[1]*
>
> *Thomas Moore*

When Colin realizes he is only as sick as he believes himself to be, he inspires his father to finally leave behind the dead guilt and bitter pain of Mrs. Craven's death and begin to enjoy being alive. In the end, the mystery and wonder of life Mary discovered in the garden are passed on to many others.[2]

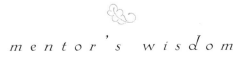

m e n t o r 's   w i s d o m

It was good for Mary to be left to herself in her new home, because it gave her something she'd never had in India—time and freedom to explore, to collect herself. With hours to spend lolling about as she chose, Mary discovered she preferred the fragrant picturesque out-of-doors to the stifling confinement of parlors and nurseries. Before long, Mary found food for her soul in the garden—a place of harmony and mystery. She found something she enjoyed—digging in the dirt, planting seeds and bulbs, dreaming of emerging beauty to come.

Gardening feeds the spiritual life, engaging the nurturer in the process of life, from the tilling of the soil to the reaping of the harvest. For Mary, the garden was a quiet, peaceful place of solitude where slow growth took precedence over the busyness of her former active but empty life. As the newly transplanted girl nurtured her dormant plot of ground, the garden rooted itself in Mary's heart. With the passage of time, her growing love of life began to spread contagiously to those around her like English ivy climbing a brick cottage wall.

Has there been a "garden mentor" in your life? He or she will be a person who listens attentively to you, provides a safe place for you to be left alone in silence, trusting that the good seeds will take root. Someone who is deeply convinced of his or her own intrinsic value, and out of that rich soil, provides a space for you to find your unique path of growth. Such a person leaves you feeling restored, beckons you to a life of joy and fruitfulness, and inspires you, in due season, to become a catalyst for others.

Mentors of inspiration come in all shapes and sizes, themselves in various seasons of life. A dear grandmother or nurturing aunt, a patient teacher, or a best friend might have been such a mentor to you. Children can be stimulators of growth, leading us by the hand, helping us find the key to living life with more gusto, with a deeper sense of gratitude. Like red-breasted robins flitting from post to post, they show us the way.

Who among us has not seen a young couple come alive with joy when a long-awaited baby is finally added to their family? Or a person who once seemed to lack the will to live suddenly begin to see each day of life as the precious gift it is, through a child companion's eyes?

My husband and I once saw this happen when a four-year-old girl named Tracy literally brought her daddy back to life. Tracy's dad and mom, Ron and Sada, were a Jewish Christian couple we met in a small fellowship group at a church we attended years ago. Ron struggled with frequent bouts of depression; Sada was a young nursing student at the time. Tracy, with ringlets of natural curls cascading down her back and eyes that twinkled with delight, appeared to be the family's joy in life. "Mama! Papa!" she often called to her parents. "Come and see! Come and see! Quick!" Describing sights, smells, and tastes we grown-ups took for granted, four-year-old Tracy was alert to all the wonder around her, from bugs crawling on the sidewalk to the tongue-tingling taste of cinnamon candies.

As our small group grew closer, Ron shared one evening about the break in relationship with his Jewish family since he and his wife had become Christians.

"My parents may never speak to me again. They say I've turned my back on them, and it's not true," Ron explained. "I love my parents. I want to spend time with them. But they won't return my phone calls when I try to explain my conversion to Christianity." Ron's voice trailed off as he wiped a tear from his eye.

The group prayed for Ron and Sada and their family. We could see no quick fixes for their finding a way to bridge the chasm between their faith in Christ and their parent's orthodox Jewish traditions. Family strife continued. One evening at our group meeting, Stan, our leader, shared an urgent concern. "Ron and Sada need our prayers desperately," Stan began. "Ron tried to kill himself this afternoon."

We were all stunned.

"It's true," Stan replied. "I knew Ron was really down about his family problems, but what I didn't know was that he lost his job two weeks ago. He and Sada kept it to themselves, but apparently Ron wasn't handling the stress well."

Ron had soaked his clothes in kerosene and set himself on fire.

"I—I can't believe this!" said one member of our group. "Why wouldn't he want to live? What would his family do without him?"

Friends reached out to Ron and Sada as best we knew how. We could only guess at what might be helpful or comforting. Time passed. Life had become so unpredictable that Ron and Sada's dream of having another child someday now sounded ridiculous.

Sada especially struggled with her mixed emotions. She was angry. How could Ron even think of abandoning her like this? She was scared. How would she support herself, her preschool daughter, and a bedfast husband? Would Ron ever work again? She was bewildered. How could he even think of leaving little Tracy without a father? It was as if Ron's spirit had died, even though his heart was still beating and his body still alive. Gangly weeds of hopelessness had invaded Ron's heart and grown to monstrous proportions, threatening to choke out his desire to live before he could hack them to the ground.

One evening while Ron was still in the hospital, Frank and I went to visit him. Ron's mother and dad, brother and sister-in-law were there visiting. The room was filled with love and laughter; forgiveness seemed to flow in abundance. It had been a close call, but Ron would recover. Life would be different from now on, though. He would be severely disfigured for life.

Frank and I moved shortly after that and lost touch with Ron, Sada, and Tracy. Occasionally we'd hear news from our old fellowship group that Ron was doing well, that he and Sada now worked on staff in the same hospital. Somehow he'd not only regained the will to live, but he'd also finished a technical course at the junior college and become a respiratory therapist.

"So tell us what happened with Ron," I asked Stan one evening when Frank and I dropped by to visit the group and renew ties with old friends.

Somehow, it had been little Tracy who had restored Ron's will to live. It may have been her bright, twinkling eyes sparkling with wonder and fascination that finally broke through her dad's depression. Or maybe her penetrating questions shook Ron's numbed spirit, sobering his thoughts and stimulating buried roots of joy and hope. "Don't you love me, Daddy? Why do you want to die? I won't let you die!"

Ron's wounded soul had burrowed deep underground, waiting in quiet numbness for a long time. But the desire to blossom and thrive returned, as perennial plants return mysteriously in due season.

In *The Secret Garden*, Mary and Colin called the energizing force that caused things to bloom "magic." In the spiritual realm, the mystery of growing—the will to live, the desire to thrive as a person—these are things that are only understood by the Master Gardener. In a way only God understands, Tracy inspired her daddy to relish life. In fact, we heard heartwarming news periodically of how well the entire family was doing. And at the appointed time, when Tracy was seven years old, a tiny bud was added to their family bouquet—little Ronald Junior.

> *I tell you the truth, unless a kernel of wheat falls to the ground and dies, it remains only a single seed. But if it dies, it produces many seeds.*
>
> Jesus, in John 12:24

LESSONS GLEANED FROM THE GARDEN

Just as there is a time for planting, germinating, and harvest, so is there also an appointed time for death. Throughout our lives, if we truly want to live fruitfully, abundantly, we will die many little deaths—deaths to self that bring life-giving results to others. In the movie *Mr. Holland's Opus,* a hopeful composer-to-be (Glenn Holland) takes a job as a high school band director. What he hopes will be a four-year stint at Kennedy High, a temporary way to make money until he can get his life-defining musical work written, turns into a thirty-year tenure at the school.

In the meantime, "life" happens, and Mr. Holland's plans are changed. His wife gets pregnant. Their child, a baby boy, has learning problems, which are finally attributed to congenital deafness. Mr. Holland, who once held a tape recording of classical tunes next to his wife's stomach to introduce his unborn son to music, now has to accept the reality that the child will never hear.

As the years pass, Mr. Holland and his wife grow increasingly distant as he becomes more frustrated, cashing in his opus for the chance to earn a living. But along the way, he discovers he has something to offer his students, and even to his son, Cole, who by this time has forged his own way as a teacher of deaf students. Although death had come to Mr. Holland's dream of composing symphonies, the joy of music was birthed in the lives of students he taught at Kennedy High.

Like seeds covered over in the dark, fertile soil, we are called to die to ourselves at times; Mr. Holland died to his dream of becoming a full-time composer of symphonies. Young mothers (and daddies) die to their need for a full night's sleep, often for months or years, to feed their babies during late-night and early-morning hours. An energetic, career-minded friend of mine recently made a choice to homeschool her children, sacrificing her personal goals to help her kids flourish. All of us have to die to the desire for immediate gratification in many ways. But these small deaths are not in vain. They become the seedlings for larger dreams, more bountiful harvests, often beyond our limited understanding.

> *It is not we who choose to awaken ourselves, but God Who chooses to awaken us.*[3]
>
> Thomas Merton

GOING TO SEED

Most of us must find contentment in knowing that our God will reap a harvest He finds fitting, even when it means dying to self again and again. Small deaths, like tiny seeds, are a part of the life cycle. Then in due season, when we lie on our deathbeds drawing our last breath, the day comes when our bodies literally go to seed, just as dried pods and seeds fall to the ground when their time of fruitfulness comes to a close.

If death approaches slowly, a gradual acceptance, and sometimes even a yearning for the next growing season, the final "coming alive," may be observed in a dying person. Even at such times as this, there is a secret in God's garden to comfort and nurture us.

My dad gave me some understanding of this final sowing of seed when the shell of his earthly body lay on a sickbed in his living room after intense suffering from cancer. Once an avid gardener, he'd loved nothing more than getting his hands in the dirt. Cultivating the earth and nurturing people had been among his areas of expertise. Those days were over now.

My mother and I cared for Dad during his six-month battle with the ruthless disease. She gave him morphine shots and sponge baths. I spooned oatmeal and Jell-O into his withered mouth and read to him. Though his death occurred over twenty-five years ago, I still remember it as if it were yesterday, so vivid is my memory of the days leading up to Dad's entrance through the hidden door of paradise.

"Sue," he'd call to me. (My dad was the only person who ever called me by my middle name, but I don't remember him ever calling me anything else.) "Sue, come and read to me," he'd say in a weak voice, patting a space on the bed beside him.

"Okay, Daddy," I'd say. I knew what he wanted to hear. It was always the same passage in 1 Thessalonians, chapter four, in these final days of his life. These were the words that often lulled him into a peaceful sleep when the morphine didn't work:

118

For the Lord himself will come down from heaven, with a loud command, with the voice of the archangel, and with the trumpet call of

God, and the dead in Christ will rise first. After that, we who are still alive and are left will be caught up together with them in the clouds to meet the Lord in the air. And so we will be with the Lord forever (1 Thessalonians 4:16-17).

In the beginning of my father's illness I'd pleaded, "O God, please don't take him. Not my dad, please, no!" I was only twenty-six at the time, a new Christian, and my preschool sons would never really know their grandpa—their wonderful grandpa. I couldn't stand the thought of his dying. But he seemed to think of death as the doorway to an ultimate "coming alive," and all he wanted to hear about was the dead in Christ rising to meet their Lord and living with Him forever and

> *As a dwelling for man, the masterpiece of creation, God designed a special place. A garden. It was an architectural triumph of both form and function, for it not only provided food and shelter for the body, it provided beauty and refreshment for the soul.*[4]
>
> Ken Gire

ever. It was the *everlasting* life following death—pushing open that final door we all have to go through to step across the threshold into the garden of eternal life—that fascinated my dad. I held his hand and stroked his arms as the life slowly drained from his emaciated body. The hazel eyes that once twinkled like stars in a midnight sky grew dim, and stilled into a steel gray silence. Then gently, quietly, Dad's spirit rose from the confines of this life.

As Mary Lennox encouraged Colin to arise and walk away from his wheelchair, an unheard voice seemed to beckon my dad home: *"Don't let us talk about dying. . . . Let us talk about living."*

w i s d o m   o f   o l d

Since the beginning of time, garden settings have come to be known as keepers of secrets and mysteries, symbolizing peaceful quietness and reflecting moments of intimacy between God and man. Early churches were often built around a courtyard garden at their center. Plots of fertile earth have also provided nurturing backdrops for significant historical events of the Christian faith.

The tree of life was planted in the Garden of Eden. After the fall of Adam and Eve, the Lord banished them from the lush setting to work the ground from which Adam had been taken (Genesis 3:23). Then God placed angels on the east side of the garden and a flaming sword to guard the way to the tree of life. The door would be open, through redemption in Christ, to again provide access to paradise.

> *Jesus said to her,*
> *"I am the resurrection and the life. He who believes in me will live, even though he dies."*
>
> *John 11:25*

In the Garden of Gethsemane, Jesus Christ became the seed to be planted in God's secret garden. Before His crucifixion, Jesus endured unspeakable suffering. Yet, knowing full well what the agony of the cross would be—the hiding of His Father's face from Him—He paid the price voluntarily, so that there could be a harvest of eternal life. How deeply, then, must it please Him when we live our lives fully, vigorously, until we draw our last breath?

Whatever the internal agonies Christ faced—the mysteries beyond our understanding—what is clear is that His death on the cross was not the end. The tomb meant to encase the shell of His dead body became, instead, the garden soil for the Seed of eternal life.

The first day of eternal springtime is not far off. In that day, at the sound of the trumpet call, this earthly life will throw off winter's white blanket, and we whose hearts belong to the Master Gardener will burst forth from the ground like lilies in April. Risen by the wounds of Christ's love. With Him, at last, in His secret garden of paradise.

Never an angel told, but this I know,
That he to whom that night Gethsemane
Opened its secrets, cannot help but go
Softly thereafter, as one lately shriven,
Passionately loving, as one much forgiven.
And never, never can his heart forget
That Head with hair all wet
With the red dews of Love's extremity,
Those eyes from which fountains of love did flow,
There in the Garden of Gethsemane.[5]

Amy Carmichael

timeless stories

of

ELDERS as MENTORS

The Velveteen Rabbit

❀

Mary Poppins

❀

Little Women

❀

The Giving Tree

❀

The Lion, the Witch and the Wardrobe

❀

Make Way for Ducklings

chapter ten

BECOMING REAL

"You become. When a child loves you

for a long, long time, not just to play with,

but really loves you,

then you become Real."

THE SKIN HORSE

The Velveteen Rabbit

by Margery Williams

The Velveteen Rabbit arrived on Christmas morning, stuffed inside the Boy's stocking. The Boy was delighted with the Rabbit, and loved him for all of two hours before getting sidetracked by other new toys and gifts. In the holiday excitement, the little Rabbit was set aside on a shelf in the toy nursery. Late at night, the toys began to move and talk. Although some of the more expensive toys in the nursery snubbed the Rabbit, the old and wise Skin Horse was kind to him.

"What is REAL?" the Rabbit asked one evening. "Does it mean having things that buzz inside you and a stick-out-handle?"

"Real isn't how you are made," answered the Skin Horse. "It's a thing that happens to you." The old horse patiently explained. "When a child loves you for a long, long time, not just to play with, but Really loves you, than you become Real." The Skin Horse himself had become real, bit by bit, because of an older boy's enduring affection. The Rabbit pondered these thoughts as the days passed.

One night the Rabbit was tucked into bed with the Boy, because the china dog he usually slept with could not be found. From that time on, the Rabbit spent long days in the garden with the Boy. He missed his wise companion, the Skin Horse. But the Boy took the Rabbit on wheelbarrow rides, and the cozy nights he spent cuddling with the Boy were so pleasant. The Boy loved the Rabbit very much. He loved the Rabbit so hard that all the pink was rubbed off his nose where the Boy kissed him.

> *It is our soul that guides us to become real, and that yearns for God and His reality and way of persistent integrity.* [1]
>
> J. Keith Miller

As time passed, the Rabbit grew shabbier and shabbier. His tail came unsewn, and his brown spots began to fade. But to the Boy, he was always beautiful. To the Boy, the Rabbit had become real.

One day the Boy became ill. The Rabbit, who had been the Boy's companion through his days of scarlet fever, was now germ-laden and taken to the trash heap to be burned. As the sad little Rabbit reflected on his days with the Boy and the Skin Horse, he began to cry. But then a strange thing happened. A mysterious flower appeared where his tears fell. Out of the flower came a fairy, the nursery magic fairy, who took him to Rabbitland. At last the Rabbit could run and play like the other rabbits. Now he was real, not just to the Boy but to everyone. [2]

mentor's wisdom

"The Skin Horse was wise," says the children's classic, "for he had seen a long succession of mechanical toys arrive to boast and swagger, and by-and-by break their mainsprings and pass away, and he knew that they were only toys, and would never turn into anything else." The seasoned overseer of the nursery had been around a long time and had seen the fads that come and go. He'd learned a lot from his years of experience, and had developed keen observation skills, a tendency to reflect on the inner life, an understanding of what works and what doesn't.

What is real? This is the question the Rabbit asked the Skin Horse. What makes it happen? How does one become real? In this chapter, we'll consider these questions and take a look at a few people who have some things in common with the Skin Horse. These mentors are people who, as author Keith Miller puts it, "yearn for God and His reality and way of persistent integrity."[3] They are people who refuse to pretend, and who understand what they were made for. Perhaps someone like my own beloved mentor, Nell.

In *The Velveteen Woman,* I shared a story of a woman who taught me a lot about giving up game playing and dropping pretenses. "Nell was a remarkable woman. A *real* woman. She was witty, elegant, wild-spirited, intoxicated with life and strangely careless about death. She was a bundle of paradoxes, gulping life to the last drop like a glass of cool water, yet eager to drink the cup of death when her summons came."[4]

After a twenty-year battle with rheumatoid arthritis, I watched Nell slip away from this life at age seventy-four. With the heart of a social worker, even as she sat in death's waiting room, Nell wanted to hear about the lives of others, to pray over their concerns. Although the crippling disease had prevented her from attending church or holding a Bible in her hands for several years, it could not tear her from her vocation of prayer. Even in her last days, she listened to tapes and watched the news to stay informed and connected with people.

As I reflect back on lessons I learned from Nell, perhaps the most significant was her sure conviction of what she was made for. Nell was certain that God loved her. She knew that her illness did not mean God was mad at her, or that He was punishing her, or that He'd turned His back on her. Even when pain had been her constant companion for a long, long time, coming and going through the years, she never pretended it wasn't hurting when it was.

Nell was confident God had settled the issue of sin a long time ago at the Cross, and that for reasons beyond her finite understanding, all He wanted from her was intimate companionship. She opened her stiff-jointed, withered arms to His love each day. "Sure cures" for rheumatoid arthritis were tried now and then, mostly to appease well-meaning friends, I think. Just as the Skin Horse explained to the Velveteen Rabbit how he'd become real because of his master's enduring love, Nell knew she'd been created to be loved by her Heavenly Father. It was this love, the unconditional, never-changing, lavish love of God, that gradually turned Nell into real.

The Velveteen Rabbit became shabby and worn as time went by, but the Boy loved him just as much. A deep knowing of God's abiding affection made Nell a real lady—transparent, genuine, humble—not only to me, but to many other people as well. When her time came, she approached heaven's gates with the joy of a five year old about to take her first ride on a Ferris wheel. With a little fear, and a whole lot of anticipation, she stepped across the threshold of eternity into the arms of Jesus.

ONCE YOU ARE REAL, YOU CAN'T BE UGLY

Skin Horse mentors are truthful and wise. Their lives demonstrate the process of becoming real and the secrets of living meaningfully.

One evening in 1995, Mitch Albom flicked on his television. On

Nightline, Ted Koppel was talking with an old man named Morrie Schwartz about what it was like to die. Mitch went numb. The old man was his former sociology professor at Brandeis University, once a beloved friend. For a moment, Mitch's thoughts flashed back twenty years to those former days at the university. Morrie had always been a thinker and a doer. A fun-loving dancer, discussion group leader, thought-provoker.

If culture doesn't work, ignore it. Keep an open heart, be compassionate, and don't chase money. Morrie's wise words from years gone by echoed in Mitch's mind as he stared blankly at the TV screen.

"Morrie?" Mitch whispered in unbelief, as if trying to somehow reconnect with his long-lost friend through the television screen. Years had passed, and while Mitch had been climbing the ladder to success as a sports columnist, Morrie had fallen victim to Lou Gehrig's disease, a debilitating illness of the nervous system. As Mitch leaned forward on the couch with his chin resting on his hands, waves of guilt penetrated his heart. "Morrie, is it you?" he repeated, recalling for the first time in years the closeness they had once shared.

The commanding tone of Ted Koppel's voice drew Mitch back to the present. Like the timeworn Velveteen Rabbit waiting for the nursery magic fairy to take him to Rabbitland, Morrie sat withered in a shaggy gray sweater, talking to a national audience about his imminent death.

The next day, Mitch caught a plane to Boston. The same intensity that had quickened Mitch's steps up the rungs of the success ladder now drove him (flew him actually) to his old friend's side. He wanted a second chance at friendship.

"Mitch! My old friend!" Morrie weakly called into the receiver when *129* he heard the familiar voice on the line. With a mix of trepidation and anticipation at seeing his friend for the first time in so many years, Mitch had called from his car phone just before arriving at Morrie's house.

Thus began Mitch's second chance. Not only at friendship, but also in education—a chance to learn the lessons he'd missed the first time around at Brandeis. This time, classes were held on Tuesdays in Morrie's house, just after breakfast. As the single student enrolled, Mitch was expected to arrive at each meeting with a fresh batch of questions and depart with a good-bye kiss for Morrie. Subjects had something to do with living fully, genuinely—things like love, work, aging, forgiveness, and death. Not necessarily the happy, upbeat topics we're likely to choose when we sit around and shoot the breeze, but subjects of substance we all need to consider if we're going to live meaningful lives. Morrie offered no apologies for this, and the subject matter was not negotiable. No grades were given, no texts were required, but Mitch was to write a paper on what he learned. Thus began the writing of Mitch Albom's book *Tuesdays with Morrie*.[5]

Over the next four or five months, Morrie and Mitch had weekly discussions about the meaning of life as Morrie awaited death. As the days went by, Morrie's life poignantly illustrated his genuine commitment to the lessons he'd spent a lifetime teaching. "If culture doesn't work, ignore it." Funny thing, the wisdom Morrie most wanted to pass on to others hadn't changed much in twenty years.

Now Mitch watched Morrie give up, little by little, the independence he'd always treasured. Soon he needed help dressing and eating, then even with the most basic human functions. In our culture, adults are conditioned to be ashamed when they need help, becoming dependent on others. And perhaps the most degrading kind of dependency is having to ask someone to take care of our most intimate or personal needs. What could be more embarrassing? more shameful? But Morrie chose to ignore this cultural norm since it didn't work for him. Instead, he approached his dependency with the delight of a child.

Because he could no longer help himself, Morrie decided to enjoy the attention his caregiver dispensed—even as he changed Morrie's diapers. Most of the time Morrie good-naturedly shared his words of wisdom, even as his shriveling body grew more dependent. He was still contributing to the growth of people around him. He was giving as an adult. And taking as a child.

Morrie had literally gotten all his fur rubbed off by disease, yet even in a baby-like state near the end of his days, he demonstrated authenticity and genuineness, ignoring culture when it didn't work, living what he taught. He'd once tried to teach Mitch the value of living and loving over the frenzy of clambering for success. Mitch hadn't absorbed Morrie's lessons very well the first time around, but they were sinking in deep this time.

Even in death's waiting room, Morrie refused to pretend. To this wise mentor, isolation in dignified privacy, withdrawing from life, couldn't compare to the fulfillment of receiving love in liberal doses. When Morrie returned to the nursery, this time as an old man needing his diapers changed and his food fed to him, he refused to be ashamed of himself. He just was not about to give in to cultural pressures that interfered with his living authentically.

Wrapped in a blanket of childlike innocence, Morrie knew he was still special and unique. He knew, as did the Skin Horse, that *"these things don't matter at all, because once you are real you can't be ugly; except to people who don't understand."*

RISKING REJECTION AND BEING REAL

People like Morrie and Nell took a few risks when they let others see their shabby spots. No doubt they got some criticism from some people who didn't understand about becoming real. Although it couldn't have always been easy for these mentors to be real, it's often even harder for church leaders, pastors, and teachers to attempt to be authentic. For the most part, the church can't handle it. We can put our pastors under so much pressure to perform, to be dynamic, to be evangelistic, to have it all together, that the job description exceeds anything a regular, limited, God-created human being could possibly attain. As our heroes, they're really taking an incredible risk if they dare to share any of their own struggles and weaknesses. While we know we aren't perfect, we expect our heroes to be.

In the church, we usually have the rules and doctrines down pat, but we don't necessarily know how to give and receive love. If you're in the ministry, you know it's extremely risky to let others see that you're really pretty shabby, that your tail may have come unsewn, or your brown spots are faded. Sometimes people actually don't want to hear about what's real, even if you are willing to risk telling them about it. It may just be too scary for them to deal with.

Ever since the Fall in the Garden of Eden, men and women have been afraid to be real. We quickly cover up our worn patches because we want others to like us, to accept us, to admire us. Sometimes we even block our own awareness and pretend to be ways we are not. Why? Surely each of us can recall a time when we tried to be real, to bare our broken heart to a friend, to ask for help with a drinking problem, or accountability with temptation to have an affair. Or perhaps we were just dying inside because we'd once had an abortion and the guilt was killing us, only to be handed a list of Scriptures or quickly shut up with empty, holy-sounding words. So we pull back in defense. We don't want to be rejected. Being real is a good thing, but it's not always safe.

In *The Secret Life of the Soul*, Keith Miller takes a bold risk as he tells the touching story of how his successful career as a counselor, author, and speaker spiraled out of control and ended in divorce as he struggled to meet the demands of people and serve God. Keith couldn't understand how he, a man who had always wanted to be real, to be honest and true to everyone, could hide the truth from himself, become dishonest, and even sabotage his own life goals and career, all the while wanting deep down to know and do God's will.

There was a baffling paradox. I was continuing to lead many people to a simpler, more focused life with Christ that was evidently real and life-changing for them, yet my own life lacked clarity, and my complex schedule was suddenly a cold and prickly acid fog bank of too many things I'd agreed to do. . . . Within myself I no longer felt the self-esteem and happiness other "committed Christians" appeared to feel. Instead, I realized I was a driven and insecure person inside. [6]

What a sad and lonely experience Keith describes. Yet how common it is, and still, we don't want to talk about such things. Keith goes on to tell how he lost touch with people close to him, and when he realized the priorities he was living did not reflect a sense of commitment to God, but instead to his own career advancement, he quickly buried the flicker of awareness that he was living a lie.

Later in his book, Keith shares how he had to learn new processes for confession and forgiveness, to work with a mentor who helped him deal with his own denial, and to discover ways to love others and himself, "blending love with the process of dealing with reality." [7]

Does this story have a ring of familiarity to you? I often see pastors' wives in my counseling office with dilemmas similar to the one Keith found himself in. Their situations may result in addiction to perfection, alcohol, shopping, or some other compulsive behavior instead of divorce. But many people in ministry find it incredibly difficult to be real, even though they may look on the outside as though they have it all together. Sooner or later, we have to get back to love.

This is what it takes for us to become real: love—real love—God's perfect love that never leaves us, even when people around us may withdraw their support and care. Love that never tires of our mistakes, our endless failures, month after month, year after year. Love that lifts the drunken prostitute out of the gutter and supports her on His strong, steady arm, who never says she's betrayed Him one too many times. *When somebody loves you, really loves you, then you become real.*

wisdom of old

Nell knew she was created for intimacy with her Heavenly Father. She knew that no matter what, God loved her. Morrie wanted to give and receive love, even when it meant losing dignity and privacy. Keith Miller helps us learn that sometimes we deceive ourselves, hiding from reality, and we get hurt, or hurt ourselves as we're trying to serve God. Only the unconditional love of our faithful God is enough to lift us from the stains and scars

> *You become. When a child loves you for a long, long time, not just to play with, but REALLY loves you, then you become real.*
>
> *The Velveteen Rabbit*

of this life. And through His loving us, year after year, we grow more real.

Jesus' ministry was not to the strong—the yuppies of His day. The Pharisees and religious leaders did not understand Jesus. He reached out to the poor, the brokenhearted, the captives and prisoners. He knew it would be risky, costly for us to be His disciples. He was fully aware that the pain, loss, failures, and poor choices we would make in this life would leave us feeling abandoned, lonely, in need of comfort and reassurance.

Jesus lived out His days eating with tax collectors and talking with prostitutes, going against the grain of culture. He walked the earth as one of us, One who struggled with all the temptations we face, loving us— always loving us—just as He found us.

> *For we do not have a high priest who is unable to sympathize with our weaknesses, but we have one who had been tempted in every way, just as we are—yet was without sin. Let us then approach the throne*

of grace with confidence, so that we may receive mercy and find grace to help us in our time of need.

Hebrews 4:15-16

Jesus was 100 percent Real. In the end, the people of His day couldn't handle it. So they crucified Him. Because of God's unconditional love for all of us sinners, Jesus willingly took the wounds that we had coming. To Him, we have always been beautiful, even with our shabby, sin-scarred lives.

He loves us, really loves us, mistakes and all.

Brethren, I urge you to become like me.

Galatians 4:12a

Because of this, and for no other reason, we can become real—like Him.

chapter eleven

MYSTIQUE

"I'll stay until the wind changes."

MARY POPPINS

Mary Poppins

by P.L. Travers

hen Mr. and Mrs. Banks advertise for a new nanny to care for their children, Mary Poppins shows up at their house, Number Seventeen Cherry Tree Lane. The two oldest of the Banks children, Michael and Jane, happened to be watching out the window that day when the stiff East Wind blew in, bending the cherry trees nearly in half and fairly flinging Mary Poppins into their front yard! With a carpet bag in one hand, an umbrella in the other, the magical nanny entered the Banks home for the first time.

"How did you come?" asked Jane. "It looked as if the wind blew you here."

"It did," answered Mary, offering no further explanation. Though the Banks family didn't know it yet, such mysterious happenings were quite ordinary for Mary Poppins.

Michael and Jane were in desperate need of just the right nanny. Their father spent all his time at work, and even when he was at home his nose was always in the *Times*. And Mother was always busy with their baby twins. Yes, Michael and Jane were in need of a special nanny—someone who understood children.

Right from the beginning, Michael and Jane knew Mary Poppins was no ordinary caretaker. They looked on as Mary unloaded her bag, which appeared completely empty when they looked inside. But then Mary began pulling things out of the bag—a starched apron, a cake of soap, other personal items. Then out came larger things, including a folding armchair! Michael and Jane would not have believed it if they hadn't seen it with their own eyes. But this was just the Banks children's first encounter with Mary Poppins' "bag of tricks." She also had a bottle of medicine that appeared to change color and flavor depending on who was taking it. Pink strawberry ice for Michael turned into green lime-flavored cordial when Jane's spoonful was poured. And for the baby twins? What else—milk!

Sliding *up* the banister, having tea parties on the ceiling, and stepping into a hand-painted landscape for an afternoon picnic were among the whimsical adventures Mary shared with Michael and Jane Banks. It's no wonder it only took a few hours for the children to fall in love with the mystical nanny who perked up others around her like a cool blast of spritz refreshes a thirsty fern. Mary's stern face and strong opinions only added to her mystique. This nanny sometimes worked quite hard at appearing a quiet, orderly person, early to bed, early to rise. But even though her daily scheduled events may have been laid out in mechanical order, Mary was anything but dull and boring.

Though Michael and Jane never ceased to be intrigued by Mary's partly human, partly magic nature, they mostly just enjoyed her presence, sometimes begging a promise of their beloved nanny. "Oh, Mary Poppins, you'll never leave us, will you?"

"I'll stay till the wind changes," was the only assurance she gave, often hurrying on with, "Spit-spot, into bed!" or stories about fairyland. Michael and Jane needed no further coaxing.

Throughout Mary's tenure, Mr. Banks became increasingly attentive to his children. The once stuffy, strictly business father actually began to enjoy the delights of childhood for himself, singing with Michael and Jane, feeding the pigeons, enjoying the little things that add sparkle to life at any age. When the wind eventually slips under her Mary's umbrella, carrying her away without warning or formal good-byes, the reader wonders why *this* day was the appointed time for her departure.

Only at story's end do we realize that the wind changed directions precisely when Mr. Banks became aware of his storehouse of riches, not in the stock market, but in his very own dear children. From that point on, his obsession with accumulating money was overtaken by a growing desire to be an intimate companion to Michael and Jane.

As Mary floated away on the wings of the wind, over the housetops and trees, the children watched tearfully from the window. But their sadness was short-lived, for Mary Poppins had left them with treasures of remembrance—a compass, a picture of herself, and perhaps best of all, a father who had learned to make time for them. And so it was with joy (and perhaps a bit of lingering sadness) that Michael and Jane Banks said good-bye to Mary Poppins, the magical nanny who had enriched their lives and hearts forever.[1]

139

m e n t o r ' s   w i s d o m

The mystery of Mary Poppins has intrigued generations of grown-ups and children alike. Daring us to try to understand her magic, she entices us to take a closer look into her only piece of luggage—an empty carpet bag—as she pulls out objects of varying sizes, one after another. *How did she do that?* we wonder. Then Mary leaves us wondering what in the world is in that bottle of medicine! Floating into the air on an umbrella (to the ceiling for a tea party), and sliding up banisters, she even defies the natural force of gravity! With magical presence she blows in on the East Wind with plans to stay "until the wind changes." Mary Poppins was not exactly concrete and specific in her approach to life.

You may know a woman with a natural streak of mystique, who invites the curiosity of others around her. People like Jackie Kennedy Onassis come to mind. Though Jackie appeared to stay out of the natural limelight as much as possible, the American public never stopped wondering what she wore, ate, and thought about, or how she spent her time. Yet nobody claimed to really know Jackie, not even those closest to her.

Suddenly a sound like the blowing of a violent wind came from heaven and filled the whole house where they were sitting.

Acts 2:2

Though few of us sport such an air of natural mystique, I believe every spiritual woman has a bit of bequeathed mystery about her, because of the Holy Spirit, who resides within. Although she's not *trying* to be a woman of mystery, a spirit-led woman is never completely predictable, since her inner promptings may take a turn this way or that at His leading. She's a growing person, ever changing, though she's probably not the least bit aware of it all. The Holy Spirit, alive in us is indeed mysterious, intriguing, far beyond our control or ability to figure out.

140

THE MYSTERY OF THE HOLY SPIRIT

A mysterious being that comes and goes with the wind, possessing unpredictable, unseen powers, who sometimes defies natural forces. A description of Mary Poppins could sound amazingly similar to the coming of the Holy Spirit as described in the second chapter of Acts! Of course, I'm not implying the magical nanny is the third Person of the Trinity, but I do believe she bears some marked resemblance to the mysterious ways of the divine, sweeping into our lives with secret purposes we cannot understand. In a similar way, God the Holy Spirit moves into our daily activities and works out His mysterious plans. All the while, His hidden purposes are being accomplished.

Michael and Jane didn't always like the mystique of Mary Poppins, and there are times when we, too, may wish the Holy Spirit would be more understandable. We don't like feeling "in the dark." In our prayer lives, we prefer getting the answers we want in an easy-to-recognize form.

One of my good friends told me a story recently that illustrates this strong preference most of us have for getting our prayers answered the way we want. Guianna's five-year-old granddaughter, Meg (who lives just down the street from her), visited her on the morning following a severe windstorm. Before Meg's arrival, the two of them had talked on the phone, and Guianna told Meg that the glass top of their patio table had blown off its base and shattered. When Meg arrived at Guianna's house a little later, she walked through the house and out onto the patio where Guianna was sweeping up the broken pieces of glass.

"Stay back, Meg," Guianna warned. "I don't want you to get cuts from these slivers of glass." When Guianna finished her sweeping, she went inside, where Meg was sitting on the sofa with a scowl on her face, arms folded.

"What's wrong, Meg?" Guianna asked.

"Well," answered the tense-jawed little girl, "I asked Jesus to heal your table."

Guianna had just been given the perfect opportunity to explain to her granddaughter that God doesn't always answer our prayers as we think He will, or the way we ask Him to. Knowing Guianna as I do, I'm sure her child-sized explanation about the mystery of the Holy Spirit went a long way toward preparing little Meg for life with a God far beyond the limits of our understanding.

After listening to my friend's story, I was aware that there are times when I am still like Meg, expecting God to answer all my prayers the way I think He should. Even as an adult with a more complicated mind than Meg has at age five, I may still expect to actually understand all the workings and mysteries of God.

But sometimes, when we least expect it, our creative Heavenly Father appears to pull things out of thin air, surprising us, taking us on an endless, fascinating adventure. Even though we don't understand, there's something so intriguing about the mystique of His dealings with us, providing for us in the ways we least expect, drawing us closer to Him, and creating a sense of wonder about what He might have up His sleeve.

Another close friend, Linda, has three daughters ages six, three, and one and a half. Linda was concerned about the middle child, hoping compliant Rebecca was not being neglected in her need for individual recognition, and observing that the other two girls often got heavier doses of attention from friends and relatives. One morning as Linda and I visited over breakfast, she said, "I have been praying that God would bless Rebecca with extra time devoted just to her. I kept looking for an empty space in my schedule to spend one-on-one time with her." Linda went on to explain that a neighbor down the street who was "best buddies" with Naomi, Linda's oldest daughter, had phoned to say she and her husband were going out for pancakes and they wondered if Rebecca could accompany them.

"Just Rebecca?" Linda asked into the phone receiver. "You want to take Rebecca by herself?" A few minutes later as Linda dressed her middle daughter for the special breakfast date she recalled her prayer on her daughter's behalf. "There I was, looking desperately for a spare half-hour because I was expecting God to answer the prayer through me. I never dreamed He'd give Rebecca special attention through someone else!" she laughed. "God always keeps me guessing!"

A CLOSER WALK

If we could sit around in a semicircle and share the unpredictable ways the Holy Spirit blows into our lives, sometimes like a rushing wind and other times more like a gentle breeze, we'd inspire each other with stories of His mystique. I wish I could hear about all your personal encounters with the Holy Spirit—we each have our share. Since I have your attention, I'll take this opportunity to share with you one of the times He recently blew into my life on the wings of the wind in a winsome way.

The morning lecture I'd given at the Fredericksburg Women's Retreat had gone well, the worship music was uplifting and reinforced the retreat theme—God's unconditional love. The Holy Spirit appeared to be moving among the women; an air of openness, spontaneity, and anticipation prevailed. Even the location, a large country barn a few miles outside of town, seemed the perfect spot for the community event sponsored by a local Christian bookstore called The Closer Walk.

Just after the lunch break, a drama team of six young adults was to perform a series of brief vignettes to further reinforce the retreat theme. As I shuffled through my lecture notes in preparation for the afternoon sessions, the drama team (who called themselves "Rocks Cry Out") took their positions near the speaker's platform. Clad in jeans and denim shirts, the team used no mikes and only a few simple props, along with some soft background music for their skits and dramatically performed sign language routines.

The first two skits were touching, making a point of Christ's desire to be the focal point of our lives, the object of our heart's deepest longings. Then came the last vignette—the grand finale—and I was totally unprepared for the way its message would reach out and grab me by the heart, awakening some sleeping places in my soul, when I wasn't even aware they'd dozed off. The scenario depicted various ways we can become distracted from our devotion to God. A mother flipping through her family photo album, engrossed in child raising, to the neglect of time with Jesus. A man with remote in hand, surfing the channels to find the latest sports update or the hottest news flash. A woman recounting her achievements, admiring her Mother-of-the-Year trophy and spit-shining her plaque for years of faithful service as president of the women's ministry team. And a man pecking at his laptop computer, intent on closing a corporate deal—all examples of subtle things that can cause us to leave God out of our lives.

After each of the four team members had rather comically played out their parts, they each froze in their positions. Then a voice called out from somewhere in the background. "You shall love the Lord your God with all your heart, with all your soul, and with all your strength and with all your mind." The voice was not a harsh, demanding one. Rather, it was gentle. As each dramatist heard the Voice, he or she moved slightly, and paused reflectively. Then, with a hint of sadness, each laid aside his or her trophies of distraction.

After a few seconds of silence, a new song began playing in the background, and each of the four team members slowly started to sway to the music, then broke out in a signing routine in unison. The tune was unfamiliar to me, but the lyrics expressed a child of God's deep yearning to be drawn close to the heart of God. As the words played: *"Pull me to Your chest, let me hear Your heart beating . . ."* a haunting feeling took me by surprise, sweeping across my heartstrings like a Ghost on a mission, creating a tune of its own deep down in my soul.

144

I knew I'd become distracted from God many times throughout my life, in all the ways acted out in the drama, plus a hundred more! But the mysterious message being delivered in that moment had nothing to do with pronouncing a verdict of guilty on any of us. It had more to do with God's pursuant heart, His love for us, and His desire to be close to us. I felt a lump rise quickly in my throat, chill bumps spread across my arms and shoulders, and tears began spilling out onto my cheeks.

I was sitting so close to one of the performers, I could see that she also had tears rolling down her face, streaking her makeup and dripping off her chin as she worshiped with abandon in symbolic movement. The words, together with the beautiful signing choreography and background music, were impressive. But the "performance" was infused with a power beyond the control of the dramatists—something supernatural was happening—the Holy Spirit Himself was in our midst, awakening our deep yearnings for closeness to God.

Then the vignette was suddenly over, and the team exited the platform. Sheila, the retreat hostess nodded in my direction, cueing it was my time to begin the afternoon lecture. *Yeah, right,* I thought, trying to turn off the tears and regain some sense of composure. The Holy Spirit had

> *Two words one could never think of applying to the Jesus of the Gospels: boring and predictable.*[2]
>
> Philip Yancey

just invaded my professional space, with no regard whatsoever for my cool, calm, "under control" persona as a retreat speaker. I somehow stumbled to the podium and mumbled, "Uhhhh," (long pause) "I'm speechless." And I truly was.

We somehow made it through the afternoon sessions of the retreat, altering our course drastically to include some interactive segments, which seemed to be the Holy Spirit's bidding. All was well with Him in control. The Holy Spirit had swept in "on the East Wind," upsetting our most carefully laid plans, wowing us with His presence.

Although I treasured the experience, I'd never have picked that moment for the Spirit to touch me so profoundly. But such is the way with mystique. Unpredictable, uncontrollable, coming and going as it pleases, intriguing us, keeping us guessing. Just as Michael and Jane

Banks wondered what might happen next at Number Seventeen Cherry Tree Lane, we sat in awe of the mysterious ways of the Holy Spirit. He had spoken to each of us that day in the barn outside Fredericksburg, calling us individually nearer to the heart of God, inviting us to take a closer walk with Him.

wisdom of old

In *The Jesus I Never Knew,* Philip Yancey has a lot to say about the mystique of Jesus, the distinct personality of the Son, always in union with the Spirit and the Father.

> *The more I studied Jesus, the more difficult it became to pigeonhole him. . . . He had uncompromising views on rich men and loose women, yet both types enjoyed his company. One day miracles seemed to flow out of Jesus; the next day his power was blocked by people's lack of faith. One day he talked in detail of the Second Coming; another, he knew neither the day nor hour. He fled from arrest at one point and marched inexorably toward it at another. He spoke eloquently about peacemaking, then told his disciples to procure swords. His extravagant claims about himself kept him at the center of controversy, but when he did something truly miraculous he tended to hush it up.[3]*

We don't understand the workings of the Holy Spirit through Jesus Christ. We'd much prefer clarity. Sometimes we get really frustrated and feel as though we're groping along in the dark as we try our best to walk in His ways. Even so, His secret purposes are being accomplished, and we are intrigued, enticed by Him to come closer, to keep following and seeking. And it's the mystery of the Holy Spirit that so powerfully draws us to Himself.

Just as Jane and Michael Banks wanted to be intimate with their mysterious nanny, we want to know Jesus, the Holy Spirit, better. Michael and Jane worried that Mary would someday leave them alone, and eventually, when the time was right, she did go. There was an element of sadness in her leaving, but they now had the consolation of their father's attention and companionship.

It's different with us. The Holy Spirit will never leave His children. We can always count on an endless supply of solutions and gifts from His supernatural bag of mysterious tricks and provisions, although they may not be exactly what we wanted or hoped for. He even keeps us guessing about heaven. Think about it. Nobody has ever comes back to tell us in detail what it's like, or shown us pictures, though God could have made that happen if He wanted to, couldn't He?

The wind blows wherever it pleases. You hear its sound, but you cannot tell where it comes from or where it is going. So it is with everyone born of the spirit.

John 3:8

God must like holding back the very best part for last too. Keeping our happy ending a secret. And on that day, we will have our Father's full attention, in a way far more fulfilling than Mr. Bank's (or any other human being's) doting could possibly be. He will be our constant companion.

He's saving the best for last.

Don't you find that exciting?

chapter twelve

Νurturing

"If you feel your value lies in being merely decorative, I fear that someday you might find yourself believing that's all that you really are. Time erodes all such beauty. But what it cannot diminish is the wonderful workings of your mind—your humor, your kindness, and your moral courage."

Marmee

Little Women
by Louisa May Alcott

The well-loved story of *Little Women* begins at Christmastime, as the March sisters, Meg, Jo, Beth, and Amy, recount the blessings and miseries of their wartime poverty. With Mr. March away on military duty, Mrs. March is left in charge of the household and their four daughters indefinitely.

The story spans more than a decade, yet Mrs. March (affectionately called Marmee by her daughters) was dependably cheerful, though often serious, and dedicated to teaching her daughters general lessons and biblical truths through everyday life experiences. The family's lifestyle, rich in tradition and celebration, was always held in high esteem not only by the March clan, but also by those who knew them well.

On Christmas morning, when Marmee asked the girls to give up their much-anticipated Christmas breakfast to a poor neighboring woman with a newborn baby and six children, the March sisters good-naturedly agreed. With thoughts of the joy they'd bring to others, the sisters pitched in to help carry the baskets of food. There had been nothing at all in the house for the poverty-stricken family to eat the day before, and the children were famished. As they huddled around the fire like hungry, freshly hatched birds with beaks upturned, Meg, Jo, Beth, and Amy passed plates piled with holiday foods. In the process, their own hearts grew merry and content. "That's loving our neighbor better than ourselves, and I like it," said Meg, as they headed toward home anticipating their own breakfast of bread and milk.

Each of the March sisters was distinctly different from the others in temperament, appearance, and outlook on life. Marmee's loving instruction and training of her daughters was custom-tailored for each of them. A nurturer par excellence, Marmee understood the girls with uncanny perception and guided them in a fluid kind of way, in agreement with their natural bent, so that it almost appeared her daughters took the lead. Meg, the oldest, was feminine and pretty, and tried to lend a hand with the younger girls. Jo was an impulsive, passionate, outspoken tomboy, while Beth was shy, peaceful, and often ill. Amy, the baby in the family, was a regular snow maiden, with blonde curly locks hanging down past her shoulders. She would grow to be preoccupied with wealth and beauty during her teenage years.

Like a mother hen gathering her chicks, Marmee often called her little women to the piano for a round of singing and girl-talk. Whether the topic of the hour was a dramatic play to be practiced under the direction of Jo, a favorite story, or a letter from Father, the March home was always abuzz with lively conversation and song. Yet life was not without its typical sibling squabbles. Marmee took seriously her charge to teach her daughters the value and benefits of hard work and time management, and her authority was never in question. She was each of the girl's most trusted confidante, and they sought her commendation above all others.

When Father became seriously ill, Marmee was called away to nurse her husband. Tearfully, she pulled herself away from a lingering embrace with her daughters and gave last-minute direction to each of her girls. "Meg, dear, be prudent, watch over your sisters, consult Hannah [the maid] in any trouble. Be patient, Jo, don't get too sad or do rash things; write to me often, and be my brave girl, ready to help and cheer us all. Beth, comfort yourself with your music and be faithful to the little home duties; and you, Amy, help all you can, be obedient, and keep happy and safe at home. Good-by, my darlings! God bless and keep us all!"

During Marmee's absence, the March sisters enjoyed a variety of indoor and outdoor adventures. Laurie, the boy next door, became a good friend to them all, but especially to Jo. Then one day Beth became seriously ill, and her sisters took turns caring for her. But Beth's condition did not improve, so a telegram was sent to Marmee alerting her to return home at once. In the meantime, the girls alternately watched over Beth and paced the floor waiting for their mother, praying all the while.

Words could not describe the meeting of mother and daughters as Marmee arrived after weeks away from home. The household was once again full of genuine happiness and security. Beth did recover from her long, feverish sleep, but remained frail and weak. Mr. March returned home from the battlefield, and the entire family enjoyed a time of joyful togetherness. But after a short while, the family met one of their saddest moments when sweet Beth died.

The story ends with a sixtieth birthday party for dear Marmee. Meg, Jo, and Amy have all matured, flown from the nest they'd shared as girls. By this time, they've come to appreciate their own harvest of husbands and children. With virtue now firmly established in their character as women, the sisters gratefully acknowledge the family blessing they have received.

"I'm far happier than I deserve," says Jo, echoed by similar comments from Meg and Amy. "We never can thank you enough for the patient sowing and reaping you have done."

Touched to the heart, Marmee can only stretch out her arms, as if to gather children and grandchildren to herself and say, with face and voice full of motherly love: "Oh, my girls, however long you may live, I never can wish you a greater happiness than this!"[1]

mentor's wisdom

What a nurturer Marmee was. With patience and wisdom she lovingly tended and trained her daughters, pointing out hazards and pitfalls along the way, as they journeyed toward maturity. Marmee was an expert at weaving virtue into the fabric of her daughters' character by engaging them in girl-talk. Amazingly, even when her little women made mistakes, Marmee avoided shaming, keeping instruction in a positive light. Sometimes her wise words were subtly threaded into conversations over the kitchen sink as she and her girls peeled potatoes, or around the piano as the quartet of sisters clustered beside their mother to sing or celebrate a special occasion.

Did you have that kind of relationship with your mom? (Remember that Marmee is a storybook character, so if your mom was like her, you're definitely in the minority.) But even if we did enjoy a wholesome, loving relationship with our mothers, we still need other caring people—mentors who nurture us, seek to understand us, and patiently bring out the best in us. Nurturers see our natural bent and direct us in ways that allow us to flourish. They are what author Marsha Sinetar calls "artists of encouragement" in her book *The Mentor's Spirit*.[2]

Marmee was a classic artist of encouragement, often giving general instruction that applied to all of her daughters. We find her addressing time and again topics like physical beauty and wealth, which she knew would challenge her daughters' value systems throughout life.

If you saw the recent film version of *Little Women*, you may recall the warm, touching scene when Marmee is sitting on a bed brushing Meg's hair, and Jo is draped across the bed. The three of them are involved in a conversation about physical appearance, and Meg, confused about the pursuit of beauty, has come to the age of hoping to meet the man of her dreams. She's been taught that outer appearance is not as important as inner virtue; yet she's noticed she can turn the heads of young men when she's all dressed up and looking her prettiest. Meg likes the attention her good looks are drawing, and she wonders if it's wrong to try to be beautiful; and if so, what makes it wrong. Pretty good questions, I'd say.

Mrs. March stops brushing Meg's hair, pauses to collect her thoughts, then voices to her daughters this timeless definition of beauty that all young women in our culture desperately need to hear:

> *I only care what you think of yourself. If you feel your value lies in being merely decorative, I fear that someday you might find yourself believing that's all that you really are. Time erodes all such beauty. But what it cannot diminish is the wonderful workings of your mind—your humor, your kindness, and your moral courage. These are the things I cherish so in you.*[3]

Marmee plumbed the depths of each daughter's soul, reading her potentials, needs, and vulnerabilities, detecting her character treasures, and bringing them all to the surface. She listened attentively to her girls, as a group of sisters and one-on-one, exploring their interests, and sometimes feeling compelled to issue a caution.

One evening, when the house was quiet, Marmee called Jo to her. Earlier that day, Amy and Jo had nearly come to blows. "It's my dreadful temper," Jo lamented. "I try to cure it; I think I have, and then it breaks out worse than ever. Oh, Mother, what shall I do? What shall I do?"

153

"Watch and pray, dear; never get tired of trying; and never think it is impossible to conquer your fault," encouraged Mrs. March, kissing Jo's cheek so tenderly that Jo began to cry.

Oh, how we all long for that kind of comfort and nurturing from our moms. From anyone! And once we've known such an artist of encouragement ourselves, we're likely to become one someday too. Someone who reaches out in a deeply caring way, possibly even altering the course of another's future by listening carefully, perceiving another's needs and potential, and drawing out the beautiful hidden treasure.

SEEING BENEATH THE SURFACE

Dorothy was a young lady in need of someone who had the ability to see her inner beauty. She needed a Marmee. This story about Dorothy is excerpted from a book called *The Blessing* by Gary Smalley and John Trent. The setting is an introductory speech class on the first day of school. The teacher asked the students to introduce themselves and respond to the questions "What do I like about myself?" and "What don't I like about myself?"

At the back of the room, nearly hiding, was a girl with long, red hair hanging down around her face, almost obscuring it from view. This was Dorothy. When her turn came to introduce herself, a silence fell over the room. The teacher moved his chair over near Dorothy, thinking that perhaps she had not heard the question. He gently repeated his words of instruction. Again, there was only silence.

Finally, with a deep sigh, Dorothy sat up in her chair, pulled back her hair, and revealed her face. Covering nearly all of one side of her face was a large, irregularly shaped birthmark—almost as red as her hair. "That," she said, "should show you what I don't like about myself."

The teacher, moved with compassion, leaned over and gave Dorothy a hug. Then he kissed her on the cheek where the birthmark was and said, "That's okay, Honey, God and I still think you're beautiful."

Dorothy began to cry, sobbing uncontrollably for almost twenty minutes. Students gathered around her to offer comfort. When she finally could talk, as she wiped the tears from her face, she said, "I've wanted so much for someone to hug me and say what you said. Why couldn't my parents do that?"[4]

This classroom teacher saw beyond the birthmark on Dorothy's face and with a simple nurturing gesture applied the healing balms of love and acceptance. He saw Dorothy as the beautiful and valuable person she truly was. Can you identify with Dorothy's longing to be nurtured, to be accepted and valued as a person worth caring for? If you can relate more to Dorothy than you can to the March girls, you're not alone or without hope for finding the nurturing you need to thrive.

Caring people are all around us, if we're on the lookout. And as I said before, once you know one, you're likely to become a life-affirming influence to others someday as well. You may find her in a kind, older woman. Or your nurturing mentor might turn out to be someone younger than you, who has developed a skill or expertise in some area you want to learn about.

AN ARTIST OF ENCOURAGEMENT

The first time I met Becky was at a writers conference held in a local church. She was the seminar leader, and I cornered her at the close of the session to ask some specific questions. After talking with her personally, I had a desire to become friends with Becky, as well as learn the ropes of the writing world.

"I don't really have a lot of time to help people get started," she said. "But occasionally, I get a sense that God has sent someone across my path, someone with the gift of writing, for the purpose of helping them get started. At such times, I try to do all I can." Secretly hoping I might be such a person, I invited her to my house for our first one-on-one get-together. She'd offered to take a look at some of the musings I'd recorded in journals over the past twenty years. In my heart, I'd always had a hidden desire to write. But the process of getting something published overwhelmed me, so I'd never pursued it.

Becky accepted my invitation, and that day at my house she became my friend and mentor, even though she was a good fifteen years younger than I.

> *Anyone who intuits our life's essential vision or themes and somehow affirms these so that we reach out for them is an artist, an artist of encouragement.* [5]
>
> Marsha Sinetar

"You have a gift," Becky announced after reading a piece I'd written about a significant life experience. "You need to share this."

"Do you really think so?" I asked, awestruck at this expert's assessment.

"Oh, yes, Brenda," she affirmed. "You need to write."

With just the right combination of challenge and reassurance, Becky fed me bites of encouragement as I handed over a series of fledgling attempts to say something meaningful on paper. *She must see some ability in me I'm not aware of,* I often mused.

"Oh, this is so good!" she said one day, briefly glancing up at me as we sat at a booth in Applebee's eating Chinese chicken salads. During those days, our girl-talk usually swirled together stories about our marriages, kids, current events, places we'd like to go, music we enjoyed, and anything else that seemed important at the time.

"Now, here." Becky pointed to a paragraph on my notebook page. "Here, you need to slow down," she said, drawing out the word *slow*. "Set the scene for the reader. What did the place look like? What sounds were you aware of? Draw me into the story with you."

Since critique is a vital part of the writing process, I tried to adopt a healthy learner's attitude and to view my mistakes as lessons that would only help build my skills. (That sounds easy and obvious enough, but receiving a writing critique on something you've worked really hard at can be sort of like having someone tell you your baby is ugly!) Becky had a way of mixing instruction with tenderness and empathy. She seemed to remember that she was once a beginner herself.

Becky became my Marmee mentor, patiently explaining the do's and don'ts of Writing 101. "Good job!" she often said. "Keep writing!" And I did. Things which were once only dreams suddenly started becoming reality, all because of the life-giving words of a nurturer.

SOUL MIRRORS

Under Becky's guidance I put together a book proposal, then she mailed copies to several publishing houses. Two of them responded, expressing a strong interest. They wanted to see more of my work. So I wrote more, and Becky encouraged me with supportive guidance and critique. Over the next few months, Becky would finalize terms for a book contract with a publishing house. Thus my first book, *The Velveteen Woman,* was conceived.

They are outer reflections, mirrors, if you will, of some vital life force already within us.[6]

Marsha Sinetar

About a year and a half after I met Becky, she hosted a get-together at Mary's of Puddin' Hill, a cozy hometown tearoom. Becky had called the meeting to pass along details about an upcoming writers conference, and she thought each of us might enjoy meeting other women who shared our affection for word-crafting. Gracie, one of the women in the group, thought it would be interesting to hear how each woman got to know Becky. So we took turns telling our stories about how we came to know our mutual mentor.

"Becky helped me find a publisher," said Kali. "I didn't have a clue where to start, and she opened the door for me to make contact with an editor."

"I couldn't believe Becky's patience as she helped me write and re-write my part of the manuscript for *Courage for the Chickenhearted*," said Suzie.

"I've just been offered my third book contract!" Annette chimed in. "Becky is the one who helped me get started."

I sat amazed as I listened to story after story of Becky's mentoring ways. Like grown-up little women, we'd gathered gratefully around our nurturing Marmee to recount the joys of growing our books. Then, at the appointed time, Becky had gently nudged each of us from the nest to fly on our own. Here we were, finding our way, eager to sing the praises of the person who first blessed us as authors in a way perhaps nobody else could have.

"You all have God-given talent," she said tearfully, in response to our plaudits. "I just drew out the gift that's been there inside each of you all along."

Touched to the heart, Mrs. March could only stretch out her arms, as if to gather children and grandchildren to herself and say, with face and voice full of motherly love: "Oh, my girls, however long you may live, I never can wish you a greater happiness than this!"

wisdom of old

158   I hope you have found a nurturing mentor—an encouraging teacher, a friend like Becky, or perhaps an older woman who lovingly instructs you, teaching you the ways of godliness. If so, you are on your way to men-toring others, as well. We need to realize that none of us has a mother with all the virtues of Marmee. She's an idealized model, a storybook mentor. But she can offer us hope for leading a life of blessing, whether

or not we had a thriving relationship with our own moms. For you, a nurturing mentor may be someone like the older woman described in the second chapter of Titus:

> *Reverent in the way they live, not to be slanderers or addicted to much wine, but to teach what is good. Then they can train the younger women to love their husbands and children, to be self-controlled and pure, to be busy at home, to be kind, and to be subject to their husbands, so that no one will malign the word of God (Titus 2:3-5).*

Doesn't she sound a lot like Marmee?

Your nurturing mentor may be older than you or younger. You may find him or her in a classroom, a hospital, even a vocational workshop. Wherever we find mentors, they'll be tenderly caring for others around them, discovering hidden potential and beauty and lovingly drawing it out.

Your beauty should not come from outward adornment. . . . Instead, it should be that of your inner self, the unfading beauty of a gentle and quiet spirit, which is of great worth in God's sight.

1 Peter 3:3-4

"Do you love me?" Jesus asked His disciple Peter (John 21).

"Yes, Lord, You know that I love You," Peter answered.

"Feed My lambs," was Jesus' instructive response.

I believe this is what nurturing mentors are doing—feeding God's lambs. Giving them what they need to reach their potential—a hug, a critique, a tableside chat—all the while tenderly caring for and encouraging their sheepish apprentices. A nurturing mentor, finding herself lovingly cared for, provided for, blessed by God, longs to pass on the divine blessing given supernaturally to her—the blessing of a Father's love. Sometimes it's given through writing lessons. At other times, through a classroom question-and-answer session.

Who is to say where a nurturing mentor will be found? But be on the lookout, because somebody in your own circle of acquaintances may be longing, at this very moment, for just such a relationship with a Marmee. Who knows? It may even turn out to be you!

chapter thirteen

JOY OF GIVING

"Come, Boy, come and climb up my trunk and swing from my branches and eat my apples, and play in my shade and be happy."

The Giving Tree

The Giving Tree

by Shel Silverstein

The Giving Tree loved a little boy, and found her deepest joy and fulfillment in giving to him, with no thought of what the boy would ever be able to give in return. Throughout the boy's childhood days, the tree lovingly shaded him. The boy climbed the tree's trunk, swung from her branches, and ate her apples. The boy loved the tree and the tree was happy.

As time went by, the boy grew up and went away. But periodically, he came back to visit the tree. When the tree grew older, she found other ways to give the boy her gifts. When the boy needed money, the tree gave him her apples so he could sell them for profit. This, too, made the tree happy. The boy went away again, and when he came back, he wanted a house. The tree then gave up her branches so the boy could build his house. Once again, the tree was happy to give unselfishly.

Then the boy went away for many, many months. The tree missed the boy. When the boy returned, the tree was overjoyed to see him. The boy wasted no time before making another request. "Can you give me a boat?" The Giving Tree gave all she had left—her trunk. The boy made a boat and sailed away.

Many years later, the boy (now an old man) returned to the Giving Tree—or what was left of her. "I wish I had something to give you. I have nothing left," the tree said to the boy. "I'm just an old stump."

As it turned out, that was all the old boy wanted now. Just a quiet place to sit and rest. And the tree stump was perfect for sitting and resting upon.

Once again, the tree was happy.[1]

m e n t o r ' s   w i s d o m

The Giving Tree gives us a glimpse of Christ, who for love sacrificed all that He had so that we could live. Though all people will fall far short of Christ's model as a Giving Tree, there are those few in this world who find their deepest joy in giving from their hearts. Drawing their nourishment from the rich soil of God's love, they aren't expecting anything in return for the gifts they give. For them, fulfillment is giving.

Have you had some "giving trees" along your path to maturity, people who bore fruit in your life, who helped shade your way at a time when without them you might have starved or scorched to death? Or who helped you build boats of hope to sail away toward a new dream when an old one died? Giving Trees are people with the ability to instinctively tune into your deepest needs, always offering refreshment as you sit in their nourishing presence.

SHARE YOUR BANANAS

In a featured interview in *Clarity* magazine, author Anne Lamott talked about a valuable lesson on giving. Anne was in San Diego doing a book tour when she saw a picture of Koko the gorilla, who lived at the San Diego Zoo. Underneath the picture were printed these words: "Mantra for the American jungle: Remain calm and share your bananas."

Anne loved this saying so much she wrote it on her hand to remind herself of her personal ministry philosophy. "What's going to last is what you give away," said Anne. "When you do God's work, you just show up and love and serve. Go take care of God's other children. Share your bananas. That's where you're going to get happy."[2]

Whether it's bananas, apples, or something else you've got to share, the point is that you give it to those around you so everybody has some, and nobody starves. It's inspiring to read about the lives of famous authors like Anne Lamott, who shared her fruit, or saints like Mother Teresa, who gave to the poor people of the world in the name of Christ.

> *Take my apples, Boy, and sell them in the city. Then you will have money and you will be happy."*
>
> *The Giving Tree*

If we're on the lookout, we'll also find Giving Trees right in front of us, friends we can actually observe, a neighbor down the street, a coworker at the office. Whom do you know that generously shares the fruits of his or her life, even motivates others to become a Giving Tree, with their only pay-off the sheer joy of sharing? Perhaps they've sheltered you from some of the emotional storms of your life, or you've watched them donate life-giving compassion and encouragement to others.

There are also those Giving Trees who give generously from their material wealth. I learned a lot about this during the years I was a single mom. Trying to support my two sons and myself on the secretary's salary

I earned at a Christian school wasn't easy. There was always a meal on the table in the evening, and I kept up with mortgage payments, but the "extras" I'd once taken for granted now became luxuries.

One early spring day in the high school office, Sandy, a close friend and coworker, watched my son Brent and three of his buddies talk excitedly about the sixth-grade wilderness trip near the Buffalo River. The sign-up (and pay up) deadline was that afternoon.

"Oh, Mom, can't I please go on the trip?" pleaded my eleven-year-old son, with sad, puppy-dog eyes. "Please?" What's a mom to do when there are bills to pay, and the school trip costs ninety dollars? There are priorities in life, right? I knew this, but it was still almost more than I could bear to see Brent left behind, excluded from an adventure the elementary students in that school looked forward to all year.

"I don't see how you can go, Brent," I managed to say, as a lump rose in my throat. "I'm sorry, but I just can't afford it."

"Hurry up, Brent, let's go outside!" shouted Clint, as I breathed a sigh of relief to be rescued from the reality of the moment. With the boys out of sight, I headed for the ladies room to see if my mascara had been smeared by a couple of tears that spilled out before I could stop them.

Unbeknownst to me, Sandy, who sat at a desk a few feet away from mine, had overheard our conversation. A generous friend, Sandy loved to shop for bargains and raid garage sales, and she'd often picked up more than she needed and shared the surplus with me. A new set of sheets from Tuesday Morning. Six boxes of Hamburger Helper from the grocery store. "It was on sale," she'd say when I protested.

When I returned from the ladies room, I noticed a lavender Kleenex neatly folded on my desktop, as if concealing something about the size of dollar bills. Picking it up, I unfolded the tissue to find four twenties and a ten. *Sandy! You can't do this!* I thought. By this time, there was no need to try and fix my make-up. A mixture of tears and mascara streamed down my cheeks. Walking over to Sandy's desk, I saw that her purse was not there.

"Have you seen Sandy?" I asked another co-worker.

"Oh, she just left," came the response. "She had carpool today."

The next morning when I approached Sandy, she busied herself with some papers. "Sandy, I tried to catch you before you left yesterday. Why did you put that ninety dollars on my desk?"

"What ninety dollars?" she asked. "Did someone give you money?" I knew this was just Sandy's way of making things a bit more comfortable for me, so I didn't push it. But in my heart, I gratefully rejoiced, thanking God for this generous friend who made it possible for my son to go camping with his classmates when otherwise he'd have been left behind. Giving Trees take no notice of what they will get in return for their gifts. In fact, some even seem to draw more joy from their generosity when they know for sure there's no chance whatsoever of a payback.

DONORS OF LIFE-GIVING LOVE

A lover of young children, Charles became an elementary school guidance counselor in his mid-forties. If you're a mom of sons, you probably know what a rare treat it is to have a *male* counselor at your kids' school. Though my sons were fully grown, I enjoyed keeping in touch with Charles, a friend and mentor I worked with in years past.

One day when I was running some errands in Dallas, I had an extra hour, so I drove over to McWhorter Elementary School to look in on Charles (Mr. Rhodes, to the children).

"It's so good to see you," Charles said, hanging up the phone receiver. "How can I help you today?"

"I'm just dropping by for a visit," I said, as someone knocked on the door. A man wearing a maintenance uniform stuck his head in.

"Just wanted to tell you the fertilizer's in the shed now," the man said, smiling.

"Oh, thanks, Jim, for picking it up," replied Charles, turning his attention back to me. "That's Jim. He's assisting the Chairman of the

Sixth Grade Fertilizer Committee."

"Fertilizer Committee?" I asked, puzzled.

"Didn't you see the landscaping on the way in?"

"Landscaping?" I asked, admitting my oversight.

"Oh, yes! All the pretty flowers! You mean you didn't see them?" He pushed himself to his feet. "We've got just two more flowerbeds to plant. Come on, you've got to see this!"

Charles had organized an elaborate garden project, complete with Compost Committee, Bulb and Seed Committee, and Irrigation Committee. He'd given different jobs to each grade level, hoping to add some little splashes of color to the elementary years of these children. Their bright smiles were the only return he wanted to receive for the investment he made in their lives.

Charles's deepest reward was seeing people around him grow and gain hope for their future, and he was willing to do all he could toward this end. After surveying the landscaping project, Charles and I returned to his office and seated ourselves in his leather chairs.

> *For however many years I am given, I give myself to you. I offer you my service and leadership, my energy, my gifts, my mind, my heart, my strength, and yes—my limitations. I offer you my self in faith, hope, and love.*[3]
>
> Cardinal Bernardin

After a few minutes, the phone rang. "Hello? . . . Oh, hi, Melba . . . Yes, okay . . . And not only that, I'll say a prayer for you today . . . Good talking to you, Melba. You take care," he concluded the brief conversation, jotting a note on a scrap of paper. "That woman's granddaughter was one of our students last year," Charles said. "This fall, she went on to junior high."

"Uh-huh?" I coaxed him to tell the rest of the story.

"Well, Melba is nearly seventy years old now. Supporting and raising a granddaughter can't be easy at her age."

"Oh, you're right, she's got her hands full," I agreed.

"So she calls me up once in a while to check in and tell me how things are going. Maybe it will help her a little if she has someone to talk to."

> *Come, boys and girls, come and swing from my branches, and play in my shade and be happy.*
>
> *The Giving Tree*

There was little doubt in my mind that this connection with someone who understood children so well was a frequent boost to Melba, and even offered spiritual support to her.

I was seated in a chair opposite Charles's desk, laden with papers and books. While he'd been talking on the phone, I noted an enlarged black-and-white photograph of two young boys in worn overalls, tattered shirts, and bare feet. It was a childhood picture of Charles and his older brother in front of their small frame house in a rural Texas town. That photograph was his way of offering hope to the children he worked with. By showing young students the poverty he'd come from, Mr. Rhodes hoped to encourage children in this lower economic neighborhood to apply themselves and set their education goals high.

Over the years I'd known Charles, I had observed him to be a man deeply rooted in the soil of biblical truths, service to God, and devotion to family, as well as dedication to helping people in his circle of influence. Those who embody the true spirit of *The Giving Tree* are rooted in the something deeper than their own personal resources—the Spirit of God Himself.

169

ROOTED AND GROUNDED IN LOVE

He is like a tree planted by streams of water, which yields its fruit in season and whose leaf does not wither. Whatever he does prospers.

Psalm 1:3

We've all heard and read stirring stories about Mother Teresa, the saint who gave all her time and energy to the poor people of India, keeping nothing for herself. Certainly she was one of the world's most generous Giving Trees, and one we will continue to learn from for many years to come.

Having observed the spiritual poverty in America, Mother Teresa was convinced that fulfillment comes from sharing, not hoarding. With smiling eyes that crinkled in the corners, she spoke openly about the Land of Plenty, where Americans have so much, but only want more. She believed that riches, both material and spiritual, could choke people who do not know how to use them fairly. Instead of collecting money and houses full of beautiful furnishings (or even minds full of facts and information they don't use), she encouraged poverty and emptiness, since our Lord would not fill hearts already brimming over.

In her book *No Greater Love,* Mother Teresa tells of how she offered her love to people around her wherever she was, knowing the recipients of her kindness could give nothing in return. This is ultimate human love—"not to be loved by anybody, not to be wanted by anybody, just to be a nobody because we have given all to Christ."[4] In giving to others, Mother Teresa was actually giving away the very essence of who she was, in order to serve God. "Jesus gives me the opportunity to feed Him by giving to those who are hungry, to clothe Him by clothing those who are naked, to heal Him by caring for those who are sick, and to offer Him shelter by housing those who are homeless and unwanted."[5]

Cut down my trunk and make a boat. Then you can sail away and be happy.

The Giving Tree is about finding real, lasting, deep joy in giving away everything one has, from a heart grounded in love. The Boy wanted apples, the Tree gave him apples. The Boy wanted a house, the Tree gave him a house. The Boy wanted a boat, the Tree gave him wood to build a boat.

Like the Giving Tree, Mother Teresa found her greatest joy in giving to others, because in so doing, she was actually giving to Jesus. The people needed a bowl of soup, Mother Teresa gave them a bowl of warm porridge. The people around Mother Teresa needed a loving touch, she reached out and touched them with the love of Christ.

Even though true Giving Trees aren't expecting anything in return, the circle of blessing has a way of multiplying itself. Those who give freely, for the joy of it, end up on the receiving end of blessings. When Henri Nouwen asked Jean Vanier, Canadian founder of a worldwide network of communities for mentally disabled people, how he found the strength to see so many people each day and listen to their many problems and pains, this was Vanier's reply: "They show me Jesus and give me life."[6]

I believe this is the secret antidote to burnout in Christian ministry—recognizing the refreshing glimpses of Christ one receives in return when he or she freely

> *A generous man will prosper; he who refreshes others will himself be refreshed.*
>
> *Proverbs 11:25*

gives to others. True ministry is not a one-way deal where self-sufficient leaders condescendingly "serve" spiritual babies, and it all stops there. We're all Giving Trees in one way or another, giving and receiving from each other's resources. Even when Giving Trees expect nothing in return, blessing the lovable and the unlovable, a generous gift comes back to them. As a byproduct, their hearts are filled full with the pure joy of God.

> *This is what God does. He gives his best—the sun to warm and the rain to nourish—to everyone, regardless: the good and the bad, the nice and the nasty. Live out your God-created identity. . . . Live generously graciously towards others, the way God lives toward you.*
>
> Matthew 5:45-48 (TM)

w i s d o m   o f   o l d

Giving Trees ultimately lead us to the Cross. After giving away all the fruits of His life, on a hand-hewn and roughly nailed-together cross, Jesus died for sinners like you and me. His only joy was in knowing that because of God's gift of salvation, something that stripped Jesus of both life and dignity, believers could one day "sail away and be happy" with Him in eternal paradise.

And perhaps most amazing of all, God made absolutely no demands in return. Not only did He give His Son Jesus, He also gave us the lavish gift of choice. Choices, choices, and more choices. The gift of choosing whether or not we will place our faith in Him. The gift of choosing how we will live, how we will spend time and money, what our priorities will be. He provides a plan for us in His Word, yes, but He does not force us to follow it. Each day we make many choices, and in each one of them we receive a priceless gift.

> *The God of our fathers raised Jesus from the dead—whom you had killed by hanging him on a tree.*
>
> *Acts 5:30*

On and on goes the giving from the heart of our loving God.

And He is pleased in the giving itself.

Even though it cost Him everything.

Have I been so long time with thee
And yet hast thou not known Me?
Blessed Master, I have known Thee
On the roads of Galilee.

Have I been so long time with thee
On the roads of Galilee:
Yet my child, hast thou not known Me
When I walked upon the sea?
Blessed Master, I have known Thee
On the roads and on the sea.
Wherefore then, hast thou not known Me
Broken in Gethsemane?
I would have thee follow, know Me
Thorn-crowned, nailed upon the Tree.
Canst thou follow, wilt thou know Me
All the way to Calvary?[7]

Amy Carmichael

For God so loved the world that he gave his one and only Son, that
whoever believes in him shall not perish but have eternal life.

John 3:16

chapter fourteen

REDEMPTION

"When a willing victim who
had committed no treachery
was killed in a traitor's stead. . .
Death itself would start
working backwards."

A s l a n

The Lion, the Witch, and the Wardrobe

by   C.S.   Lewis

Peter. Lucy, Susan, and Edmund go to stay as houseguests of a kindly professor in one of the Chronicles of Narnia, *The Lion, the Witch, and the Wardrobe.* This allegory about the struggle between good and evil waged within the human spirit explores the ways of the heart, and how redemption is possible through the power of active goodness and redeeming love.

In the professor's mysterious old country house, Lucy is the first to stumble through the back of an enormous wardrobe, entering the secret country known as Narnia. When Lucy returns from her exploration, she tells her siblings about the secret land, but they don't believe her. A while later, however, Edmund also finds his way through the dark, wooden wardrobe, into the land of Narnia. *So Lucy* was *telling the truth after all,* Edmund says to himself.

Soon after entering Narnia, Edmund encounters the White Witch. Although he does not initially intend to do evil, the vulnerable and naive Edmund has difficulty controlling his appetite for the wicked witch's savory delicacy, Turkish Delight, and is sent by his own passions on a course of selfish pursuit.

In Narnia, a dramatic struggle between good and evil is being played out. When the children arrive, the friendly Mr. and Mrs. Beaver tell them that when two sons of Adam and two daughters of Eve (two human boys and two girls) enter Narnia, this is the sign that the great lion called Aslan is returning to reclaim his kingdom.

> They say Aslan is on the move," said Mr. Beaver.
>
> "Who is Aslan?" Susan asked.
>
> "Aslan? Why He's the King," replied Mr. Beaver. "He's the Lord of the whole wood."
>
> "Is he a man?" asked Lucy.
>
> "Aslan a man! Certainly not. Aslan is a lion—the great lion."
>
> "Ooh!" said Susan. "Is he—quite safe? I shall feel rather nervous about meeting a lion."
>
> "Safe?" said Mrs. Beaver. "Who said anything about safe? 'Course he isn't safe. But he's good. He's the King, I tell you."

Aslan is the redeemer mentor in this story who will come to save Narnia from the White Witch. Under her rule, Narnia is condemned to a state of perpetual winter with no Christmas.

Edmund, the prodigal child, wants to believe the White Witch is actually good. For a while, he believes her promises to make him a prince, and keep him supplied with all the Turkish Delight he wants. After Edmund has sold his soul to the White Witch unaware, it becomes his duty to surrender his brothers and sisters to her. When he cannot, the witch orders servants to prepare Edmund as a victim for slaughter. Meanwhile, Aslan rescues Edmund. But the witch reappears with her army, demanding the traitor's blood.

"You have a traitor there, Aslan," says the witch.

"His offense was not against you," answers Aslan.

"Have you forgotten the Deep Magic?" taunts the witch. "You know that every traitor belongs to me as my lawful prey and for every treachery I have a right to kill. . . . His blood is my property."

"It is very true," says Aslan. "I do not deny it."

Aslan offers himself up to the witch in Edmund's place. He is shaved, muzzled, and laid on the Stone Table. But he returns the next day, alive and well. The children are confused.

"Though the witch knew the Deep Magic, there is a magic deeper still which she did not know," explains Aslan. "If she could have looked a little further back, she would have known that when a willing victim who has committed no treachery was killed in a traitor's stead, the Table would crack and Death itself would start working backwards."

Narnia is freed, the White Witch dies, and Aslan departs, only to return later for a season of celebration. "Edmund the Just" is restored to a place of favor and crowned king along with his brother and sisters, who remain kings and queens forever. The children then return safely to the professor's home through the wardrobe. So ends this adventures in the enchanted world of Narnia.[1]

mentor's wisdom

Aslan depicts with clarity the sacrifice Jesus made for all of us sinners when He died on the cross. Shorn of His glory, rights, dignity, life itself, He offered Himself up for the redemption of all who would accept Him. Then, like "Edmund the Just," we are declared just because, and only because, Jesus Christ has redeemed us.

Although no human beings possess the capability to take another's place in the way Christ did, there are people in our lives who offer a kind of redemptive influence. These are people who suffer or sacrifice so others won't have to, or who pay a debt another person cannot pay, as Aslan laid himself on the Stone Table because Edmund could not surrender his brother and sisters to the White Witch. Perhaps you are even such a person yourself. Victor Hugo's classic, *Les Miserables*, poignantly illustrates what can result when one person offers a kind of redemption to another.

Jean Valjean, poor, starving Frenchman, is sentenced to serve five years in a brutal prison for stealing a loaf of bread. But his sentence is extended by his several attempts at escape, and eventually he serves nineteen years of hard labor. When he is finally released, the "yellow passport" he must carry and display, identifying him to all as a dangerous ex-convict, prevents him from receiving food and shelter. Hardened by his years in the harsh prison, desperate to survive, Valjean steals from a bishop who has given him supper and a clean bed to sleep in. When Valjean is caught with the silver plates hidden underneath his clothes, the authorities bring him to the bishop to confirm their suspicion that he has stolen. But to Valjean's amazement, the bishop covers for him by saying that the silver was a gift. After the officers leave, the wise old priest goes to the kitchen cupboard and withdraws the silver candlesticks. "Here. Take these as well," he says, handing them over to Valjean.

"What are you doing?" Valjean asks, stunned and confused.

"Go, my brother," says the bishop. "You no longer belong to evil, but to good. It is your soul I am buying . . . and I give it to God!"

For the rest of his life, the grateful Jean Valjean graciously doles out generosity to others, passing on to all who enter into his path the love and goodness once shown to him by the old parish priest. The priest is a life-changing mentor to Jean Valjean, in the same way Aslan was a redeemer to Edmund.

When we begin to see the magnitude of our redemption through Christ, His lavish love offered to us, we want to love others who, like us, don't deserve it. Just as Jean Valjean's hardened heart softened and he became compassionate to others because he received so much, we also want to pass on the grace given to us through our redemption in Christ.

But in this world, there are things that keep us from becoming redeeming mentors for others. Sometimes we don't see our own evil. At first, the White Witch seemed kind and generous to Edmund, freely giving him his fill of tasty Turkish Delight. Even when Lucy told Edmund about the evil spell of perpetual winter the Witch had cast over Narnia, he still wanted to believe the witch was good. Like Edmund, we may see our own actions as quite reasonable.

THE POWER OF SELF-DECEPTION

When we do wrong, we usually find out soon enough and repent and get back on track. But when we do good, become pleased with ourselves and receive applause and commendation from our leaders and friends, we easily lose our sense of dependence on God and our always and ever increasingly desperate need for grace.[2]

Eugene Peterson

Much has been written about obvious sins, but I think it's those insidious sins masquerading as "good deeds" that really trip us up. Like saying you're sharing a prayer request with several women friends, when you're really just spreading gossip, violating another's trust. Or (this one may nab more men than women) like a workaholic spending twelve hours a day, six days a week at the office for weeks on end telling himself that this is giving "faithful service" to the company or the church.

At what point does apparent good become a masquerade for evil? Is there a clear line of demarcation in every case? I don't think so. It seems to me we're a lot like Edmund, starting out with good intentions, but

179

indulging just a bit here and there in the delectable treats of this world, like recognition at our jobs, status in the church, things like that. Before we know it, we're hooked into our boss' expectations, the needs of the women's ministry committee, and we've lost our freedom. And all the while, we were just trying to be good.

I have referred to the story of the Prodigal Son previously in this book, noting the father's unconditional love as a type of Christ's love. In this chapter, however, I'd like to switch the focus a bit and take a closer look at the two brothers. You recall that in the story, the younger

> *The devil is fighting with God, and the battlefield is the human heart.*[3]
>
> *Fyodor Dostoevsky*

brother is sent by his own passions on a course of selfish pursuit. He goes to a faraway country, where he squanders his money and then returns to the father, who graciously reinstates him with full rights as a son.

Bad, bad boy, we may say to ourselves. *He didn't deserve it*. The younger brother's sin is glaringly obvious. But it's easy to peruse this story and miss the evil in the older brother's heart. Cloaked in self-righteousness and a sense of dutiful loyalty, he first appears obedient, virtuous. He's the one who stayed at home to serve his father faithfully. And yet in his reaction to his brother's homecoming, we see evidence of festering anger, jealousy, and resentment.

"Look! All these years I've been slaving for you and never disobeyed your orders. Yet you never gave me even a young goat so I could celebrate with my friends. But when this son of yours who has squandered your property with prostitutes comes home, you kill the fattened calf for him!" (Luke 15:29)

The older brother was the family hero, the praised brother, the one who did good things. But in spiritual terms, he became just as "lost" as the younger brother. While the young son sank to the level of a pigsty, the older boy fell into the mire of envy.

There are occasions when all of us are like the older brother, and at other times we may identify more strongly with the younger. But whether we're examining ourselves or observing others, we're more likely to be duped by evil that looks like good on the outside. And we can only live out of gratitude when we acknowledge our need for forgiveness and grace for what we are inside. As Eugene Peterson said, "In the Christian life our primary task isn't to avoid sin, which is impossible anyway, but to *recognize* sin."[4]

This tendency to become deceived about sin, especially in ourselves, is further illustrated in the Gospel of Luke. One evening, one of the Pharisees asked Jesus to come over to his house for a meal. As they sat down at the dinner table, a woman of the village, the town harlot, came with a bottle of expensive perfume and knelt at Jesus' feet, bathing them with her tears, drying them with her hair, and anointing them with perfume. Simon, the Pharisee, was disgusted that Jesus would let such a woman touch Him. Jesus then told this story.

> *Two men were in debt to a banker. One owed five hundred silver pieces, the other fifty. Neither of them could pay up, and so the banker canceled both debts. Which of the two would be more grateful?"*
>
> *Simon answered, "I suppose the one who was forgiven the most."*
>
> *"That's right," said Jesus. Then turning to the woman, but speaking to Simon, he said, "Do you see this woman? I came to your home; you provided no water for my feet, but she rained tears on my feet and dried them with her hair. You gave me no greeting, but from the time I arrived she hasn't quit kissing my feet. You provided nothing for freshening up, but she has soothed my feet with perfume. Impressive, isn't it? She was forgiven many, many sins, and so she is very, very grateful. If the forgiveness in minimal, the gratitude is minimal."*

Luke 7:41-48 (TM)

The harlot's sins were obvious, while the Pharisee's were hidden,

181

especially to himself. "The subtlety of sin is that it doesn't feel like sin when we're doing it; it feels godlike, it feels religious, it feels fulfilling and satisfying."[5]

You have a traitor there, Aslan," says the witch.

"I do not deny it," says Aslan.

In one way or another, we are all traitors who deserve to be butchered on the Stone Table. If we want to become redeeming mentors, we must realize that try as we will, we cannot *avoid* sin. Instead, we need to shift our focus to being open to *recognizing* the evil in our hearts. "Search me, O God, and know my heart; test me and know my anxious thoughts," prayed the psalmist (Psalm 139:23).

Our own sins won't be obvious to us. But as we sit with God in quietness, He will faithfully show us the evil in our actions and motives, and give us the strength to face our own internal ugliness. Unless we are willing to see the evil in our own hearts, we think we deserve Christ's love. But none of us does. If we can face the truth of our imperfection and receive God's unmerited favor for ourselves, then we are free to pass on God's love to others. Then we are on our way to becoming redeeming mentors.

It's not easy to become this kind of mentor. It takes divine revelation and God's strength to face up to the evil within our hearts. But if we ask God to help us, as the psalmist did, He will do it, and not always in the same way for everyone. A friend named Marianne once told me a story of how she became a redeeming mentor, forgiving others when they didn't deserve it, all because she took a long, hard look at the evil inside her own heart.

FORGIVENESS AND REDEMPTION

Although Marianne and her family lived in the same Dallas suburb Frank and I lived in, she had somehow learned to live quite peacefully in the midst of the hustle and bustle of the city. I knew that her life hadn't been easy, and one evening I asked her how she'd managed to attain a genuinely peaceful spirit in the midst of life's storms.

"What helped me was coming to the full realization that God is the only One who is pure Goodness. Every person, including myself, is both good and evil at times," she said.

As I stared at my friend, puzzled, Marianne went on to explain that a relative in their family had molested her two daughters while they were quite small. She had responded by trying her best to protect them, homeschooling the girls through high school and closely supervising all their activities.

"Looking back, I now see that I actually thought I could protect my daughters *myself*." With the help of a trusted Christian counselor, Marianne's daughters worked through the trauma of their childhood abuse. The three of them even became active in volunteer work in the Crisis Pregnancy Center during the girls' high school years. Then, while away at college, the older daughter was tragically raped. "I saw only failure and fear in Ginny's future," Marianne confided. "I angrily shouted at God one day, 'I turn my back for just one moment, and look what happens? Is this how You care for my children? And You expect me to forgive that horrible, evil person?' "

The heart is deceitful above all things.
Jeremiah 17:9

Marianne found that even when she took lots of precautions about her children's safety, she could not ultimately protect them from the evils of this world.

"But what was it about this horrible experience that led you to see God's redeeming goodness in all of this?" I asked, probing deeper. I didn't want to miss even a smidgen of this woman's wisdom.

"One day," Marianne went on with her explanation, "I was standing in the shower, and I became intensely aware of my hate for Ginny's abuser."

183

"Hate, did you say?" I asked, interrupting again.

"Yes. Pure hate. God's presence became apparent, and this question came to mind: *What do you want Me to do to him, Marianne?*"

So I answered out loud, in the shower: "I'd like to claw his eyes out! I wish huge chunks of skin would just fall off his body."

As Marianne recited her hate wishes to God, an image of the boy who abused Ginny came into her mind. "I saw his body the way I described it—with large chunks of flesh just hanging off his bones. As I stared at it, his body slowly transformed into an image of Jesus."

Marianne went on to say this was God's way of showing her that *He* had already taken all the wounds Marianne wanted to inflict on the boy. *Jesus* had laid Himself on the Stone Table in the boy's place; He had taken all those marks of hatred and shame, not only for the boy, but also for Marianne. By this time, Marianne had recognized the deceptive evil in her own heart, as well as the sin of her daughter's perpetrator. All the sins of the world had already been paid for, because of God's redeeming love.

> *The sweet sound of amazing grace saves us from the necessity of self-deception. It keeps us from denying that though Christ was victorious, the battle with lust, greed, and pride still rages within us.*[6]
>
> Brennan Manning

My friend's eyes glistened as she concluded the story about the day in the shower and how a horrifying experience had only confirmed in her heart that although she intended to be on good behavior at all times, pleasing God, sometimes she herself was evil, unaware.

As the months passed, Marianne's daughter saw the change in her mother's heart. As far as they knew, the perpetrator never came to repentance. Ironically, in the end, it was Marianne's daughter who benefited most from her mom's redemptive attitude.

wisdom of old

Rise up and help us; redeem us because of your unfailing love.

Psalm 44:26

All of us will experience various temptations in this life. One man or woman's Turkish Delight may be vanity, pride, or sexual vulnerability. Another may be enticed by the overwhelming tendency to gossip. The form is not what matters—some sins look virtuous to us. But God sees the White Witch for who she is—Satan enticing us with sin, disguised as delectable Turkish Delight. The truth is, each of us is part good and part evil. Ultimately, only a holy God can pay for our sins.

In our world, as in Narnia, a dramatic struggle between good and evil is being played out. Each of us, with prodigal hearts, is sent from time to time by our own passions for love, success, or power, on a course of selfish pursuit. Often we don't feel safe, even when we belong to God. Sometimes life even seems like a perpetual winter during which Christmas never comes.

But He entered the Most Holy Place once for all by his own blood, having obtained eternal redemption.

Hebrews 9:12

But on the Cross, Christ died for our redemption. Since all humans are traitors—part good and part evil—only a holy Christ could pay the debt we owed. Jesus Christ was the shorn lamb laid on the Stone Table in our place, for the sins we could never pay for. At that time, the power of death over us was reversed. And instead of the condemnation we deserve, we will one day reign in the heavenlies as sons and daughters of our Redeemer.

Who is this Christ the Redeemer?

Why, He's the King, I tell you.

185

chapter fifteen

HOMEMAKING

"*Take good care of the ducklings.*

I'll meet you in a week."

Mr. Mallard

Make Way For Ducklings
by Robert McCloskey

hen the busy streets of Boston proved to be a dangerous place for raising ducklings, Mr. and Mrs. Mallard decided they'd have to find a safer nesting spot. They looked at Beacon Hill and around the State House in search of a place suitable for raising their wee webbed ones.

"That island looks like a nice quiet place," said Mr. Mallard, spying a secluded spot amongst the bushes near the water. Mrs. Mallard agreed, and the two ducks settled down to build their nest on the bank of the Charles River. In their new home, Mr. and Mrs. Mallard met Michael, a friendly neighborhood policeman who fed them an endless supply of peanuts.

One day Mr. Mallard decided to take a trip to explore other places along the river, ever in search of the ideal family home. "I'll meet you in a week, in the Public Garden," he quacked over his shoulder. "Take good care of the ducklings." Of course, Mrs. Mallard knew all about bringing up children. She taught the ducklings how to swim and dive, walk in a line, and keep away from bikes and scooters. Jack, Kack, Lack, Mack, Nack, Ouack, Pack, and Quack lined up and followed Mrs. Mallard everywhere she went.

After a week passed, Mrs. Mallard and the ducklings traveled through the city on their way to the Public Park to meet Mr. Mallard. But when they came to the busy cross streets, cars began honking at them. Michael came to their rescue and enlisted the help of several police-men. Traffic was held back so the Mallards could cross the street, then march on to their appointed meeting place in the Public Park.

As promised, Mr. Mallard was there waiting for his family. After just a few days, the Mallards decided they liked the island in the Public Park so much, they decided to make it their permanent home. Here, the ducks found a haven of safety, comfort, and peace, where they enjoyed them-selves, swimming about, following the swan boats, and eating peanuts all day long.[1]

m e n t o r ' s   w i s d o m

Mr. Mallard was always scouting out new frontiers in search of the best home he could find for his duckling clan, while Mrs. Mallard stayed with the children, feeding them, giving them lots of love and lessons in swim-ming and safety. Our storybook mentors, Mr. and Mrs. Mallard, worked together to keep all their "ducks in a row." Only the safest, most secure, and comfiest nest would do for their family.

Some of you may be settling your own "nest" at this time, preparing a place of warmth, safety, and security for raising children. Or you may be at the other end of the child-raising continuum, discovering the fulfillment of an empty nest. Some may be grandmothers raising grandchildren, fluffing up your nest to include unexpected guests because, for whatever reason, their moms and dads are unable to provide for their kids. Maybe you never found the right "Mr. Mallard." Or you got married, but the loving and stable relationships you hoped for with the people in your nest have not worked out so well.

If you are in the minority of people who look back on a happy childhood in a secure home, and even in your adult life the traditional family scene has worked out well for you, praise God. But family roles and structures have changed a lot over the past two or three decades in our country, and most of us now find ourselves in quite non-traditional nests.

Regardless of the place you call home at this time in your life, if it's functioning pretty well, there is a central person, a homemaker, who sort of holds it all together. He or she is the person who takes care of you, who can be counted on to give you a snuggly hug, a pat on the back, or a listening ear. Someone also works hard to make money to buy the house, furnishings, and clothing for the family. Since the making of a home involves all of this and more, things run a lot more smoothly if there are two adults sharing the workload the way Mr. and Mrs. Mallard did.

Yet, even with the best efforts of the strongest homemakers, there are times when something happens, and our security is threatened in some way. A woman loses her husband through divorce or death. Or a couple can no longer pay the mortgage on their house, and are forced to move their nestlings into a small apartment.

In the simple children's story *Make Way For Ducklings*, Mr. Mallard decided to move the family nest because the streets of Boston were so busy. Safety was missing. He never stopped scouting out the riverbanks and nearby parks in search of a better home for his ducklings—someplace more comfortable, safer, and more secure, where his family could enjoy a fulfilling life.

In a much more profound way, a true story is told of Jesus, the Maker of our eternal home, who has gone on ahead of us to prepare our place in heaven. In our eternal home, nothing at all, not a single thing, will be missing. We will at last find the safety and security we have always been looking for. All of our heartaches will finally be soothed.

But in the meantime, while we're on our journey through the busy streets of this world, I believe there are some ways we can find encouragement, even in the midst of all that is missing in our homes and relationships. There are a few Mallard mentors who can help us find our way. They teach us that although we can't find all the joys of heaven in this life, we can bring Jesus into our daily environments as our unseen host, making our life experience here as rich as possible. Have you found some meaningful ways to gather your family or friends together in your home or apartment to share the blessings of God? I recently read an inspiring story about a sixty-year-old woman named Gena, who used her alternative nesting skills to create a home for the down-and-out.

MARTHA STEWART DOESN'T NEST HERE

The setting is a dark, brick building on Mount Eden Parkway in the Bronx, where Gena provides food and clean beds for the homeless. Come-and-go boarders are expected to show respect for God as the unseen host in this house for as long as they stay.

"If they a Muslim, I say what happened to Allah when you needed a bed?" declared Gena. "Is he on vacation? Is he asleep? When you in my God's house, eating my God's food, you show Him respect."

A sign above the door reads, "This is a drug-free building. Violators will forfeit their freedom." The house rules make no allowance for drugs or sexual activity between guests during their time of residence.

"I ain't never put nobody out. You put yourselves out," Gena says. This homemaker aims to foster responsibility, decency, and respect for the host-behind-the-scenes, her Lord Jesus Christ. Homemaking is Gena's vocational calling. "God better call you to this, I tell you one thing, or the devil will kill you in a minute," she says. "You cain't be wanting anything or depending on anything but the name of Jesus in this business, no sir. We on the straight and narrow, honey. When you on this road, you gotta grease down."

> *One day Mr. Mallard decided he'd like to take a trip to see what the rest of the river was like, further on. So off he set.*
>
> Make Way for Ducklings

Gena's family members say that her heart has always been soft. Throughout her life, Gena has offered a home to the helpless and hopeless, even though it never earned her much praise. "They say, 'Give me breakfast, and hurry up!' I don't feel sorry for them. I am motivated by Jesus Christ. If I wasn't, I'd throw water in their faces."[2]

This woman has found a way to pick up the slack for down-and-outers, creating a nest for those who would otherwise not have a home. To do this, she scouted out the neighborhoods in the Bronx, found a suitable building, and began providing all the missing elements of home: shelter, food, safety, house rules—literally everything needed for the fortunate ones who would come to stay with her.

THE MAKING OF A HOME

> *I will not leave you orphaned. I'm coming back. In just a little while the world will no longer see me, but you're going to see me because I am alive and you're about to come alive. At that moment you will know absolutely that I'm in my Father, and you're in me, and I'm in you."*
>
> Jesus, in John 14:18-20 (TM)

191

Did your childhood home offer the things Gena provided for her houseguests? Was there someone who enforced reasonable rules? Someone who prepared meals, supplied comfort, made money for food and clothing?

Was your home a warm place of safety and security? What was missing?

When I was a little girl growing up in a small agricultural town in California, my mother worked six days a week as a grocery store checker, my dad as an auto mechanic. My fondest memories are of times with family when Mother was at home. When she had the time, she could stir up some delicious concoctions in the kitchen, sending savory smells wafting throughout the house.

Our living room was the center of our home, furnished with a watermelon-red chenille sofa, Dad's overstuffed leather rocker, and a couple of chartreuse occasional chairs. (The colors sound pretty wild, but they were popular and really classy in the fifties.) A mahogany buffet was stacked high with cold cuts and hard-crusted rolls on New Year's Day, Mexican hors d'oeuvres and homemade fried apricot pies on Christmas Eve, and other snacks as the occasion called for throughout the year. (Remember, I said my mother worked in a grocery store, so there was always plenty of food.)

On Saturday nights during my growing-up years, my sister and I cooked hamburgers just before Mother arrived home from work and Dad came in from his usual afternoon therapy session in his garden. Then we'd get out the TV trays, load up our plates with hamburger fixings and potato chips, grab a glass of iced tea, and settle into our living room nesting places and watch "Flipper." It was our Saturday night ritual. Not only did we always have plenty of food, we sometimes hung out together as a family, watching television or playing cards.

Yet, even with all the things my parents worked so hard to provide as homemakers, I grew up with a sense of hollow emptiness in the place I called home. It felt like something, or someone, was missing. I had no real understanding or appreciation of my parents' needs and values, or their reasons for working so hard outside our home. At that time, I didn't know how to understand what kept my own "Mrs. Mallard" away from our nest so many hours, or how to put my feelings into words. But I longed to spend time with my mom, baking cookies, sewing, learning to make a flower arrangement, or just reading a story together.

Years later, I realized that creating a beautiful, well-maintained home with nice furniture and impeccably kept flower gardens was vitally important to my parents, since they'd grown up in the lean years of the Depression. I had to do a lot of growing up myself before I could realize that for my parents, providing material things was the ultimate way they tried to show love to their nestlings.

If you grew up in poverty, you may not feel much sympathy for my childhood feelings of loneliness in the midst of plenty of material stuff. You may have longed for new dresses, a pretty doll, or enough food to eat. For some of you, the place you called home was a place of pain and abuse. You may even bristle when you hear stories of hearth and home at all. None of us had a perfect childhood home. There was always something missing.

LONGING TO BE LOVED

Cassandra was a high-spirited adolescent. Her parents brought her to counseling because they'd caught her sneaking out of the house at night several times. Their family story was pretty typical. Cassandra felt that her parents didn't care much about her, that they were overly strict and wouldn't listen to her. So she'd started climbing out her bedroom window after dark to

> *Home is Christ's kingdom, which exists within us and among us as we wend our prodigal ways through the world in search of it.*[3]
>
> *Frederick Buechner*

go to the park to meet a boy who paid attention to her and made her feel desirable, worth knowing, worth spending time with.

"I won't quit seeing him!" she shouted at her dad during our second counseling session. "He's the only person in the whole wide world who even knows I exist!"

"Don't you talk to me like that, girl," her red-faced father yelled, pointing his finger in her face.

I could see it was time to initiate some principles for more effective communicating, which I did. But something deeper was going on with this girl. She was trying to express a soul hunger that far surpassed stringing words together in a coherent way. Yes, Cassandra definitely had some behavior problems. She was defying the authority of her parents and disobeying their rules.

Yet, after hearing her heart longings, I realized they weren't really much different from those I hear from many Christian women, nor from my own. Cassandra just wanted a meaningful connection with someone who thought she was beautiful and desirable. To sit with someone who would see her, hear her, value her, acknowledge her thoughts and feelings. Isn't this what we all want?

I once thought men were far more prone to sexual temptation than women, but my experience as a counselor of women has taught me this is not the case. While men are attracted to beautiful ladies with voluptuous bodies, women are often vulnerable to emotionally responsive men. Sometimes when women

> *The heart of the father burns with an immense desire to bring his children home.*[*]
>
> *Henri Nouwen*

find things missing at home, if they can't get their man's attention or he won't talk to them, they may also sneak out of the house after dark like Cassandra did, hoping nobody will notice they're gone. They may climb out the window to take a trip to the mall for a spree of out-of-control shopping. Or they may sneak food into their bedrooms so they can binge on it later, or they may find themselves in the arms of another man.

Don't get me wrong. I'm not condoning defiant behavior in adolescents, or extramarital affairs in the lives of women. I'm only recognizing the longing we all have to feel validated and worthwhile. We yearn for completeness that even the best of marriages on earth cannot entirely fulfill. We need something more. We need to find a way to meaningfully connect with Jesus, the lover of our souls.

AT HOME IN YOUR HEART

How do you deal with your longings for what's missing in your home? in your life? in your heart? What do you do with the feelings of emptiness and isolation that gnaw at you?

I am discovering that there is a better way than sneaking away from home to get what's missing in this life. And we don't even have to leave the house. We only need to look inside ourselves, in our hearts, where Christ makes His home.

> *I've loved you the way my Father has loved me. Make yourself at home in my love.*
>
> Jesus, in John 15:9 (TM)

I know of only one way to get across the busiest, noisiest streets of my world, and to find refuge from the loud honking of sin that blares at me—bitterness, greed, envy, lust. I must go to Jesus, the loving Homemaker within my heart, for only He can meet my deepest longings. Only He can soothe my emotional pains, comfort me in my losses, and provide me with the safety I need in a place I can call home.

As long as I am on my journey to the perfect island in the Public Park, where I will finally find Christ waiting for me, I will always have a need to meet with Him in the quietness of my own heart. It is here that I find a sacred time of silence, solitude, being with God, until He calls me to the eternal home he is preparing for me in heaven. I do this by setting aside my Bible study and prayer list, because as much as we need to study and pray, the part of the spiritual life we seem to most often neglect is just *being with* our Father. Yet, this is how relationships are formed and strengthened—spending quality time together—just sitting quietly with Jesus in stillness, inviting His spirit speak to me.

∽∾∽

You can do this at any time, in the quietness of your own heart, where Jesus makes His home. As you sit in His presence, what is He saying to you? Is there grief in your heart that you've never resolved? If so, let yourself cry it out. Don't hold back the tears any longer, He wants to comfort you in your sadness. Is there anger? Tell God all about it. Let the feelings just pour out. Jesus is already aware of all the pain and fear underneath the anger, you can talk to Him about it. Are you engaged in a battle with temptation? Perhaps you are in the habit of sneaking out of the house by drowning your sorrows with alcohol, compulsively surfing the Internet, or just constant busyness. In the privacy of your own heart, sit down with your homemaker and let Him comfort you, heal you, give you His blessing.

The Lord your God is with you. . . . He will take great delight in you, he will quiet you with his love, he will rejoice over you with singing.

Zephaniah 3:17

In silence, listen to the voice who calls you His beauty, His beloved, who calls you home, so He can quiet you with His love, and rejoice over you with singing. It happens in the quietness of your own heart—His home.

∽∾∽

In his book *The Inner Voice of Love,* Henri Nouwen beautifully describes his own way of meeting with Jesus, the homemaker of his heart:

You can look at your life as a large cone that becomes narrower the deeper you go. There are many doors in that cone that give you chances to leave the journey. But you have been closing these doors one after the other, making yourself go deeper and deeper into your center. You know that Jesus is waiting for you at the end, just as you know that he is guiding you as you move in that direction. Every time you close another door—be it the door of immediate satisfaction, the door of distracting entertainment, the door of busyness, the door of guilt and worry, or the door of self-rejection—you commit yourself to go deeper into your heart and thus deeper into the heart of God. You have to be willing to live your loneliness, your incompleteness, your lack of total incarnation fearlessly, and trust that God will give you the people to keep showing you the truth of who you are.[5]

Until we get to heaven, meeting Jesus in our hearts, where He makes His home, is the only way to find stillness, to cross the dangerous, busy streets of this world. Like the Mallards, we are on our way to our ideal, eternal home, where we will meet our Father face-to-face. On that day, the head of our heavenly household will welcome us into His arms, and the passionate longing for completeness we've tried so hard to find here on this earth will finally be fulfilled. At last, we will have found our perfect nesting place, where we will follow the swan boats and eat peanuts all day long.

wisdom of old

HOMECOMING

In another of Henri Nouwen's books, *The Return of the Prodigal Son—A Story of Homecoming,* Henri explains how a chance encounter with a reproduction of Rembrandt's painting of the Prodigal Son catapulted him on a long spiritual adventure. He noted that in the painting, the outstretched hands of the father were the central focal point, at least for him.

Looking at the way in which Rembrandt portrays the father, there came to me a whole new interior understanding of tenderness, mercy, and forgiveness. Every detail of the father's figure—the facial expression, his posture, the colors of his dress, and most of all, the still gesture of his hands—speaks of the divine love for humanity that existed from the beginning and ever will be.[6]

Henri said he almost titled the book *The Welcome by the Compassionate Father*. This is the Father, the loving homemaker, who will one day reach out to embrace us as we enter heaven's gates. On that day, we will know with all our hearts that even though we may have had to travel the noisiest streets through the slums of this earth, our Father has always been loving us, each step along the way, through all of life's traffic jams, always forgiving, always expectantly awaiting our homecoming.

> *The door on which we have been knocking all our lives will open at last.*[7]
>
> C.S. Lewis

Take good care of the ducklings. I'll meet you in a week!"

Yet I am always with you; you hold me by my right hand. You guide me with your counsel, and afterward you will take me into glory. Whom have I in heaven but you? And being with you, I desire nothing on earth. My flesh and my heart may fail, but God is the strength of my heart and my portion forever.

Psalm 73:23-26

We conclude this final chapter of *Storybook Mentors* as the Mallards finally find their ideal home on the island in the public park. Here they were not only safe and comfortable, they also enjoyed themselves swimming with the swan boats and eating peanuts all day long. Sounds pretty heavenly, doesn't it?

Someday we will also reach our ideal home. We don't have any black-and-white descriptions of what heaven is like, but it seems only appropriate to end this book with thoughts of home, in the tradition and spirit of childhood—seeing it from a child's point of view. Remember? We see more clearly when we look at life through a child's eyes. By now, we've learned together that a part of grown-up wisdom is reawakening our childlike qualities—imagination, love, free spirit, grace, and so much more—all the things our storybook mentors have reminded us of.

The way I sometimes picture it in my mind, when we reach heaven's gates, we'll finally be welcomed into the arms of our loving Father, the One we've been meeting with in that quiet place inside our hearts. At last, we'll see the face of our True Love, the One we've been longing for, desiring to be with, the lover of our souls.

Perhaps He'll be flanked on either side by a happy throng of welcoming saints, cheering as they wave brightly-colored streamers.

"Make way for Donna!"

"Make way for Sandy!"

> *All real art comes from the deepest self—painting, writing, music, dance. Our truest prayers come from there, too. And from there also come our best dreams and our times of gladdest playing.*[8]
>
> *Frederick Buechner*

We'll spend our days in the company of Jesus, skipping down sunlit paths in the heavenly forest, holding His hand, as we gather sparkling rocks from the bottoms of rippling streams. We'll gather pine needles all day long, weave coverlets for the birds in our heavenly home, and dance with Jesus in the moonlight. Together, we'll chase beautiful Monarch butterflies over the rocks, under the waterfalls and through the trees, and when we catch them, they'll only smile and give us butterfly kisses, and not be hurt. Jesus will be our constant companion.

And the sun will never go down.

It will be all we've dreamed of, and more.

At last, at last, we'll hear the words we've always been longing to hear.

Welcome home!

I am going there to prepare a place for you. And if I go and prepare a place for you, I will come back and take you to be with me that you also may be where I am."

John 14:2-3

Endnotes

Introduction

1 Eugene Peterson, *Leap Over a Wall* (New York: Harper Collins, 1997), 73.

2 Emily Dickinson.

Anne of Green Gables

1 Lucy Maud Montgomery, *Anne of Green Gables* (New York: Penguin Putnam, 1987). Originally published in 1908.

2 Brent Curtis & John Eldredge, *The Sacred Romance,* audiotape series purchased from their counseling office in 1998.

3 Henri Nouwen, *Reaching Out* (New York: Doubleday, 1975), 39.

4 Robert Benson, *Living Prayer* (New York: Tarcher/Putnam, 1998) 110.

5 Brent Curtis & John Eldredge, *The Sacred Romance* (Nashville, TN: Thomas Nelson, 1997), 180.

A Little Princess

1 Frances Hodgson Burnett, *A Little Princess* (New York: Harper Collins, 1963). Originally published in 1905.

2 Curtis & Eldredge, 82.

3 G. K. Chesterton quoted in Vigen Guroian, *Tending the Heart of Virtue* (Oxford, NY: Oxford University Press, 1998), 113.

4 Diane Langberg, *On the Threshold of Hope* (Wheaton, IL: Tyndale House, 1999), 17.

5 Langberg, 112.

6 Viktor Frankl, *Man's Search for Meaning* (Philadelphia: Westminster Press, 1961), 87.

Heidi

1 Johanna Spyri, *Heidi* (New York: Random House, 1998). Originally published in 1880.

2 David Seamands quoted in Philip Yancey, *What's So Amazing About Grace?* (Grand Rapids, MI: Zondervan, 1997),15.

3 Henri Nouwen, *Return of the Prodigal Son* (New York: Doubleday, 1992), 13.

4 Brennan Manning, *Reflections For Ragamuffins* (San Francisco: Harper Collins, 1998), 142.

5 Ibid.

Pippi Longstocking

1 Astrid Lindgren, *Pippi Longstocking* (New York: Viking Press, 1950). Originally published in 1945.

2 Viktor Frankl, *Man's Search for Meaning* (Philadelphia: Westminster Press, 1961), 43.

3 Eugene Peterson, *Traveling Light* (Colorado Springs, CO: Helmers & Howard, 1988), 23.

4 Thomas Merton, *New Seeds of Contemplation* (New York: New Directions Books, 1962), 131.

Pollyanna

1 Sir Philip Sidney quoted in *Kim Anderson's Daybook* 2000, copyright NBM Bahner Studios AG, 1999), pages not numbered.

2 Eleanor H. Porter, *Pollyanna* (New York: Penguin Books, 1969). Originally published in 1927 by Harrap in Great Britain.

3 Nikos Kazantzakis quoted in Sarah Ban Breathnach, *Simple Abundance* (New York: Warner Books, 1995), May 24.

4 Albert Camus quoted in Robert Corrigan, *The World of the Theatre* (Dubuque, IA: Wm. C. Brown, 1992), 109.

5 Julian of Norwich quoted in Brennan Manning, *The Ragamuffin Gospel* (Sisters, OR: Multnomah Press, 1990), 34.

Charlotte's Web

1 E. B. White, *Charlotte's Web* (New York: Harper Collins, 1952).

2 Henri Nouwen, *The Wounded Healer* (New York: Doubleday, 1979), 72.

3 Ruth Harms Calkin, "I Wonder," from *Tell Me Again, Lord, I Forget*, Pomona, CA, © 1984. Used by permission. All rights reserved.

4 Corrie ten Boom quoted in Judith Couchman, *Designing A Woman's Life* (Sisters, OR: Questar, 1995), 30-31.

The Little Engine That Could

1 Watty Piper, *The Little Engine That Could* (New York: Platt & Munk, 1930). From *The Pony Engine*, by Mabel C. Bragg (George H. Doran & Co.).

2 Bill Marvel, "Never Too Old to Learn," *The Dallas Morning News,* February 5, 2000.

3 Henry Cloud & John Townsend, *Boundaries* (Grand Rapids, MI: Zondervan, 1992), p. 100.

4 Lewis Smedes, *How Can It Be All Right When Everything Is All Wrong?* (Wheaton, IL: Harold Shaw, 1999), 104.

5 C.S. Lewis, in Wayne Martindale & Jerry Root (eds.), *The Quotable Lewis* (Wheaton, IL: Tyndale House, 1989) 209.

Black Beauty

1 Anna Sewell, *Black Beauty* (New York: Bantam Doubleday Dell, 1990). Originally published in 1877.

2 Rick Bragg, *All Over But the Shoutin'* (New York: Random House), 7.

3 Ibid., 8.

4 Ernest Kurtz & Katherine Ketcham, *The Spirituality of Imperfection* (New York: Bantam Books, 1992),186.

5 Brennan Manning, *The Ragamuffin Gospel* (Sisters, OR: Multnomah, 1990), 26.

6 Henri Nouwen, *Life of the Beloved* (New York: Crossroad Publishing, 1992), 57.

The Secret Garden

1 Thomas Moore, *The Re-enchantment of Everyday Life* (New York: Harper Collins, 1996), audiotape.

2 Francis Hodgson Burnett, *The Secret Garden* (New York: Watermill Press, 1987). Originally published in 1911.

3 Merton, p. 10.

4 Ken Gire, *Reflections on Your Life* (Colorado Springs, CO: Chariot Victor, 1998), 14.

5 Amy Carmichael, *Toward Jerusalem* (Fort Washington, PA: Christian Literature Crusade, 1977), 91.

The Velveteen Rabbit

1 J. Keith Miller, *The Secret Life of the Soul* (Nashville, TN: Broadman & Holman, 1997), 160.

2 Margery Williams, *The Velveteen Rabbit* (Philadelphia: Running Press, 1981). Originally published by Doubleday in 1922.

3 Miller, 161.

4 Brenda Waggoner, *The Velveteen Woman* (Colorado Springs, CO: Chariot Victor, 1999), 196.

5 Mitch Albom, *Tuesdays With Morrie* (New York: Doubleday, 1997), 142.

6 Miller, 11.

7 Ibid., 205.

Mary Poppins

1 P. L. Travers, *Mary Poppins* (Orlando, FL: Harcourt, Brace & Co., 1997). Originally published in 1934.

2 Philip Yancey, *The Jesus I Never Knew* (Grand Rapids, MI: Zondervan, 1995), 23.

3 Ibid., 23.

Little Women

1 Louisa May Alcott, *Little Women*, (New York: Grosset & Dunlap, 1947). Originally published in 1868-69.

2 Marsha Sinetar, *The Mentor's Spirit* (Boulder, CO: Sounds True, 1997), audiotape.

3 *Little Women*, Blockbuster Video version.

4 Gary Smalley & John Trent, *The Blessing* (Nashville, TN: Thomas Nelson, 1986). Summary of a story that appears on pp. 47-48.

5 Sinetar.

6 Ibid.

The Giving Tree

1 Shel Silverstein, *The Giving Tree* (New York: Harper & Row, 1964).

2 Mary Ann O'Roark article in *Clarity* (New York: Guideposts, February-March 2000), summary from pp. 29-33.

3 Cardinal Bernardin quoted on Sinetar audiotape.

4 Mother Teresa, *No Greater Love* (Novato, CA: New World Library, 1997), 82.

5 Ibid., 100.

6 Jean Vanier quoted in Henri Nouwen, *Here & Now* (New York: Crossroad Publishing,1994), 83.

7 Carmichael, 84.

The Lion, the Witch, and the Wardrobe

1 C.S. Lewis, *The Lion, the Witch, and the Wardrobe* (New York: Macmillan, 1950).

2 Peterson, 167.

3 Dostoevsky quoted in Vigen Guroian, 35.

4 Peterson, 186.

5 Ibid., 187.

6 Manning, *The Ragamuffin Gospel*, 21.

Make Way For Ducklings

1 Robert McCloskey, *Make Way For Ducklings* (New York: Viking Press, 1941).

2 Lauralee Mannes story, "Welcome to Sister Gena's Place," retold by Judith Couchman, 23-26. This story first appeared in *Clarity* May/June 1994.

3 Frederick Buechner, *The Longing for Home* (New York: Harper Collins, 1996), 18.

4 Henri Nouwen, *The Return of the Prodigal Son* (New York: Doubleday, 1992), 93.

5 Henri Nouwen, *The Inner Voice* (New York: Doubleday, 1996), 51.

6 Henri Nouwen, *Return of the Prodigal Son,* Boulder, CO: Sounds True, 1998, audio-tape.

7 C.S. Lewis quote in Curtis & Eldredge, 177.

8 Buechner, 17.

A Personal Note From the Author

More than to just entertain, Cook publishing hopes to inspire you to fulfill the great commandment: to love God with all your heart, soul, mind and strength and your neighbor as yourself. Toward that end, the author wishes to share these personal thoughts with you.

Heart

Recently I was discussing the simplicity of childlike faith with a group of women. "The simplest truths, like 'Jesus loves me' are the most profound," said one lady. Then another chimed in, "Yes, that's true. But although such truths are simple, they are not easy to grasp, nor easy to believe or live."

I could only heartily agree. The realities of grown-up life can complicate our faith, our ways of living with God, our approach to biblical truths. It has not been easy for me to believe the simple truths like 'Jesus loves me,' or to receive His gifts with childlike faith. (See *The Velveteen Woman*, Cook Communications.) After more than twenty years as a Christian, I began to see what it means to approach God with a childlike heart.

Soul

Storybook Mentors is written in the spirit of Matthew 18:1-4, in which the disciples came to Jesus and asked, "Who is the greatest in the kingdom of heaven?" He called a little child and had him stand among them. And He said, "I tell you the truth, unless you change and become like little children, you will never enter the kingdom of heaven. Therefore, whoever humbles himself like this child is the greatest in the kingdom of heaven."

Mind

Debbie Alsdorf has written a Bible study called *Steadfast Love*. Its focus is the unconditional love of our Lord for His children. I recommend it to you for further reading, regardless of your age, how long you've been a Christian, or how many analytical studies you have done. The grace of God is such a simple concept that we easily miss it as grown-ups, because it doesn't make any sense. But that's just the point! We need to quit trying to understand, and simply embrace God's love as a child does. I also recommend Brennan Mannings' *The Ragamuffin Gospel*, and his most recent release, *Ruthless Trust*. Brennan has the ability to cut through the ways we adults complicate the Gospel and expose the bare bones of Christ's lavish love for us. You'll be blessed!

Strength

To apply the truths from *Storybook Mentors*, try reading the chapters with your childlike heart. (Yes, it's still in there!) The mentor's lessons are simple. The plots of the stories have a lot in common with our daily grown-up dramas. you may also want to re-read a couple of your favorite childhood classics to see if new insights come to you in a fresh way.

Lord Jesus,

My deepest desire is that each reader of *Storybook Mentors* receive its words with the heart of a child—the heart You have created within her—expectant, open, with a sense of wonder, simplicity, and anticipation. Draw her back to the basic truths of Your Word, and renew her in your love. Refresh her through these simple stories and illustrations.

For Your glory, Amen.

About the Author

Brenda Waggoner lives in Texas with her husband, Frank, and their dogs, Molly and Tanzi. Brenda is a licensed professional counselor and a conference/retreat speaker. Her seminars are built around the themes of her two books, *The Velveteen Woman* and *Storybook Mentors*, both published by Cook Communicatons Ministries. The seminars are designed to encourage women who long to live genuinely, authentically, and bring the joys of childhood into their grown-up lives. To receive information on her seminars, or for details about her speaking schedule, you may write her at:

Brenda Waggoner
16301 CR 558
Farmersville TX 75442
E-mail: FBWaggoner@aol.com
            Or contact her speakers' bureau:
Speak Up Speaker Services
1614 Edison Shores Place
Port Huron, MI 48060
(888) 870-7719
E-mail: Speakupinc@aol.com